THIMBLEBERRIES®
Small Wonders

Landauer Publishing, LLC

THIMBLEBERRIES®
Small Wonders
by Lynette Jensen

Copyright © 2011 by Landauer Publishing, LLC
Projects Copyright© 2011 by Lynette Jensen

This book was designed, produced, and published by Landauer Publishing, LLC
3100 101st Street, Urbandale, IA 50322
800-557-2144; 515-287-2144; www.landauercorp.com

President/Publisher: Jeramy Lanigan Landauer
Vice President of Sales and Administration: Kitty Jacobson
Editor: Jeri Simon
Art Director: Laurel Albright
Creative Director: Lynette Jensen
Photographer: Sue Voegtlin
Technical Writer: Sue Bahr
Technical Illustrator: Lisa Kirchoff

We also wish to thank the support staff of the Thimbleberries® Design Studio:
Sherry Husske, Julie Jergens, Virginia Brodd, Ardelle Paulson, and machine quilters:
Clarine Howe and Connie Albin.

The following manufacturers are licensed to sell Thimbleberries® products:
Thimbleberries® Rugs (www.colonialmills.com);
Thimbleberries® Quilt Stencils (www.quiltingcreations.com); and
Thimbleberries® Sewing Thread (www.robison-anton.com and www.Sulky.com).

This book is printed on acid-free paper.

Printed in China 10 9 8 7 6 5 4 3 2 1

Library of Congress Control Number: 2011926247

ISBN 10: 1-935726-04-8
ISBN 13: 978-1-935726-04-3

Introduction

Ease, simplicity and classic country style are hallmarks of Thimbleberries® Design Studio. For more than 23 years, we have brought beautiful fabrics, patterns and inspirations for quilted home comforts to quilters worldwide.

Among the most popular patterns today are those that not only bring the distinctive Thimbleberries® look to home décor, but also are timeless and quick-to-complete. We recognize that a quilter's time is limited. That's why Thimbleberries has always been dedicated to satisfying a quilter's love of quilting with projects that can be completed easily and successfully.

In Thimbleberries® Small Wonders, you'll find a collection of 44 quilting inspirations, each with the clear and simple instructions that make it easy for even a beginner to enjoy.

Our thanks to you for once again welcoming Thimbleberries® into your home. Enjoy.

My best,

Lynette Jensen

Contents

table runners

Peaks and Valleys

20 x 48-inches

Fabrics & Supplies

5/8 yard **LARGE BLUE FLORAL** for runner center

1/4 yard **BEIGE PRINT** for pieced border

1/4 yard **ROSE PRINT** for pieced border

1/4 yard **GREEN PRINT** for pieced border

1/4 yard **DARK BLUE PRINT** for outer border

3/8 yard **DARK BLUE PRINT** for binding

1-1/2 yards for backing

quilt batting, at least 26 x 54-inches

Before beginning this project,
read through **Getting Started** *on page 181.*

Quilt Top

Cutting

From **LARGE BLUE FLORAL**:
- Cut 1, 20-1/2 x 32-1/2-inch rectangle for center

From **ROSE PRINT**:
- Cut 1, 5-1/4 x 44-inch strip

From **BEIGE PRINT**:
- Cut 1, 5-1/4 x 44-inch strip

From **GREEN PRINT**:
- Cut 1, 4-7/8 x 44-inch strip. From strip cut: 5, 4-7/8-inch squares. Cut the squares diagonally in half to make 10 triangles.

4-7/8"

From **DARK BLUE PRINT**:
- Cut 1, 4-1/2 x 44-inch strip. From strip cut: 2, 4-1/2 x 20-1/2-inch outer border strips

Piecing

Refer to arrows on diagrams for pressing.

Step 1 With right sides together, layer the 5-1/4 x 44-inch **ROSE** and **BEIGE** strips. Press together, but do not sew. Cut layered strip into squares. Cut layered squares diagonally into quarters to make 10 sets of triangles. Stitch along the bias edge of the layered triangles; press.

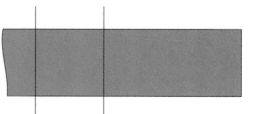

Crosscut 3, 5-1/4-inch squares

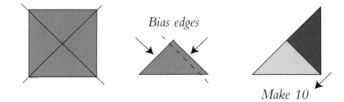

Bias edges

Make 10

7

Step 2 Sew **GREEN** triangles to the bias edge of each of the Step 1 triangle sets; press. <u>At this point each pieced block should measure 4-1/2-inches square.</u>

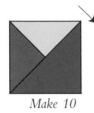

Make 10

Step 3 Sew Step 2 pieced blocks together in 2 rows with 5 blocks in each row; press. <u>At this point each pieced border should measure 4-1/2 x 20-1/2-inches.</u>

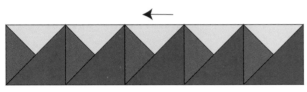

Make 2

Step 4 Sew the pieced borders to both ends of the 20-1/2 x 32-1/2-inch **LARGE BLUE FLORAL** runner top rectangle; press.

Step 5 Sew the 4-1/2 x 20-1/2-inch **DARK BLUE** outer border strips to the runner center; press. <u>At this point the runner center should measure 20-1/2 x 48-1/2-inches.</u>

Putting It All Together

Trim backing and batting so they are 6-inches larger than runner top. Refer to *Finishing the Quilt* on page 189 for complete instructions.

Quilting Suggestions:

• **LARGE BLUE** floral center - meander

• **BEIGE** triangles - stipple

• **GREEN/PINK** triangles - in-the-ditch

• **DARK BLUE** outer border
  TB31 - 3" Blossom Swirl

TB31-3" Blossom Swirl

THIMBLEBERRIES® *quilt stencils by Quilting Creations International are available at your local quilt shop or visit www.quiltingcreations.com.*

Binding
Cutting

From **DARK BLUE PRINT**:
• Cut 4, 2-1/2 x 44-inch strips.

To maintain perfect triangle tips at the outer edges, sew binding to quilt top using a <u>1/4-inch seam allowance.</u> This measurement will produce a 3/8-inch wide finished double binding. Refer to *Binding* and *Diagonal Piecing* on page 189 for complete instructions.

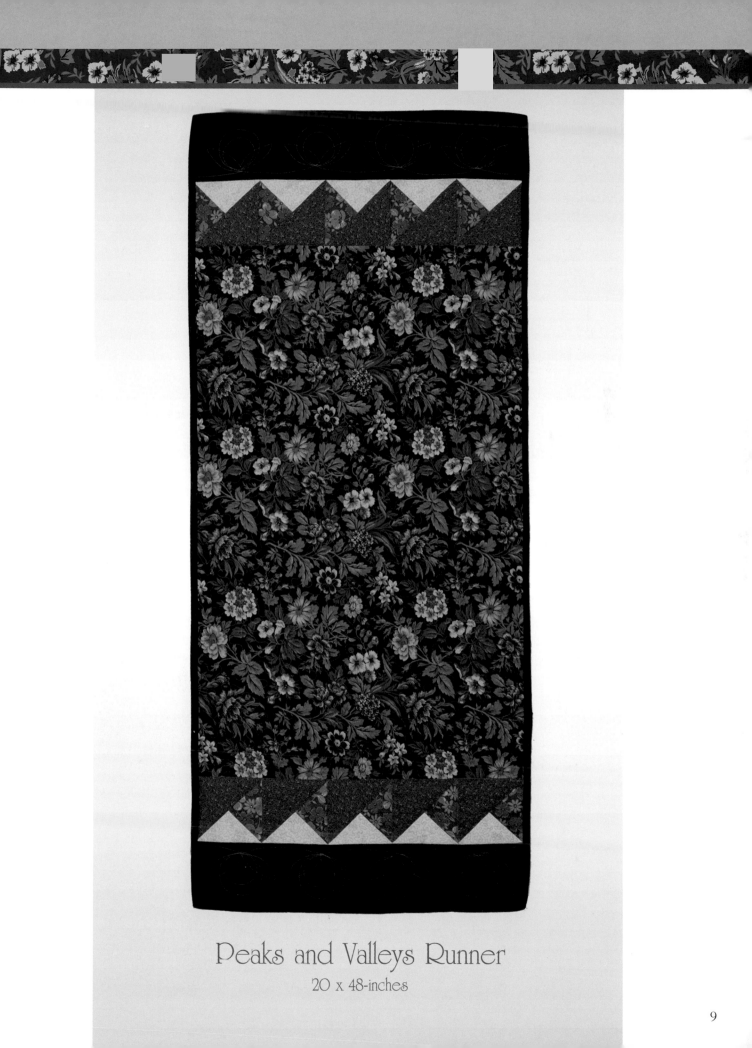

Peaks and Valleys Runner
20 x 48-inches

Cottage

14 x 30-inches

Fabrics & Supplies

1/4 yard **SALMON PRINT** for blocks

1/4 yard **GREEN PRINT** for blocks

1/4 yard **BLUE/TAN PRINT** for blocks

1/4 yard **PEACH PRINT** for blocks

1/4 yard **BLUE PRINT** for sawtooth border

3/8 yard **TAN FLORAL** for sawtooth background, outer border

1/3 yard **BLUE PRINT** for binding

5/8 yard for backing

quilt batting, at least 20 x 36-inches

*Before beginning this project, read through **Getting Started** on page 181.*

Triangle-Pieced Square Blocks

Makes 12 blocks

Cutting

From **SALMON, GREEN, BLUE/TAN,** and **PEACH PRINTS**:

• Cut 1, 4-7/8 x 44-inch strip from *each* fabric. From *each* strip cut: 3, 4-7/8-inch squares

Piecing

Refer to arrows on diagrams for pressing.

Step 1 With right sides together, layer (3) 4-7/8-inch **SALMON** and (3) 4-7/8-inch **GREEN** squares together in pairs. Press together, but do not sew. Cut layered squares in half diagonally to make 6 sets of triangles. Stitch 1/4-inch from diagonal edge of each pair of triangles; press.

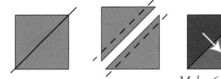

Make 6, 4-1/2-inch triangle-pieced squares

Step 2 With right sides together, layer (3) 4-7/8-inch **BLUE/TAN** and (3) 4-7/8-inch **PEACH** squares together in pairs. Press together, but do not sew. Cut layered squares in half diagonally to make 6 sets of triangles. Stitch 1/4-inch from diagonal edge of each pair of triangles; press.

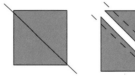

Make 6, 4-1/2-inch triangle-pieced squares

Step 3 Referring to diagrams, sew Step 1 and Step 2 triangle-pieced squares together in pairs to make 3 different units; press. Referring to runner diagram on page 12, sew the units together to make the runner center. Press seam allowances toward bottom edge of runner. <u>At this point the runner center should measure 8-1/2 x 24-1/2-inches.</u>

Unit A	Unit B	Unit C
Make 3	Make 2	Make 1

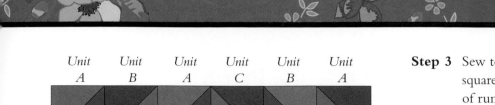

Unit A	Unit B	Unit A	Unit C	Unit B	Unit A

Runner Diagram

Sawtooth Border

Cutting

From **BLUE PRINT**:

• Cut 2, 2-7/8 x 44-inch strips

From **TAN FLORAL**:

• Cut 2, 2-7/8 x 44-inch strips
• Cut 4, 2-1/2-inch squares

Piecing

Step 1 With right sides together, layer 2-7/8 x 44-inch **BLUE** and **TAN FLORAL** strips together in pairs. Press together, but do not sew. Cut layered strips into squares. Cut layered squares in half diagonally to make 32 sets of triangles. Stitch 1/4-inch from diagonal edge of each triangle set; press.

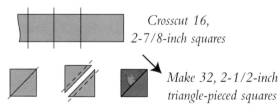

Crosscut 16, 2-7/8-inch squares

Make 32, 2-1/2-inch triangle-pieced squares

Step 2 Sew together 4 of the triangle-pieced squares; press. Make 2 sawtooth borders. At this point each border strip should measure 2-1/2 x 8-1/2-inches. Sew sawtooth borders to top/bottom edges of runner center. Press seam allowances toward runner center.

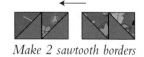

Make 2 sawtooth borders

Step 3 Sew together 12 of the triangle-pieced squares. Press seam allowances toward top edge of runner. Sew 2-1/2-inch **TAN FLORAL** squares to both ends of the strip; press. Make 2 sawtooth borders. At this point each sawtooth border strip should measure 2-1/2 x 28-1/2-inches. Sew sawtooth borders to runner center; press.

Make 2 sawtooth borders

Border

Note: Yardage given allows for border strips to be cut on crosswise grain. Diagonally piece strips as needed referring to **Diagonal Piecing** *instructions on page 189. Read through* **Border** *instructions on page 187 for general instructions on adding borders.*

Cutting

From **TAN FLORAL**:

• Cut 3, 1-1/2 x 44-inch outer border strips
• Attach 1-1/2-inch wide **TAN FLORAL** outer border strips.

Putting It All Together

Trim batting and backing so they are approximately 6-inches larger than runner top. Refer to **Finishing the Quilt** on page 189 for complete instructions.

Quilting Suggestions:

• All triangles – in-the-ditch
• **TAN FLORAL** – meander

Binding

Cutting

From **BLUE PRINT**:

• Cut 3, 2-3/4 x 44-inch strips.

Sew binding to runner using a 3/8-inch seam allowance. This measurement will produce a 1/2-inch wide finished double binding. Refer to **Binding** and **Diagonal Piecing** on page 189 for complete instructions.

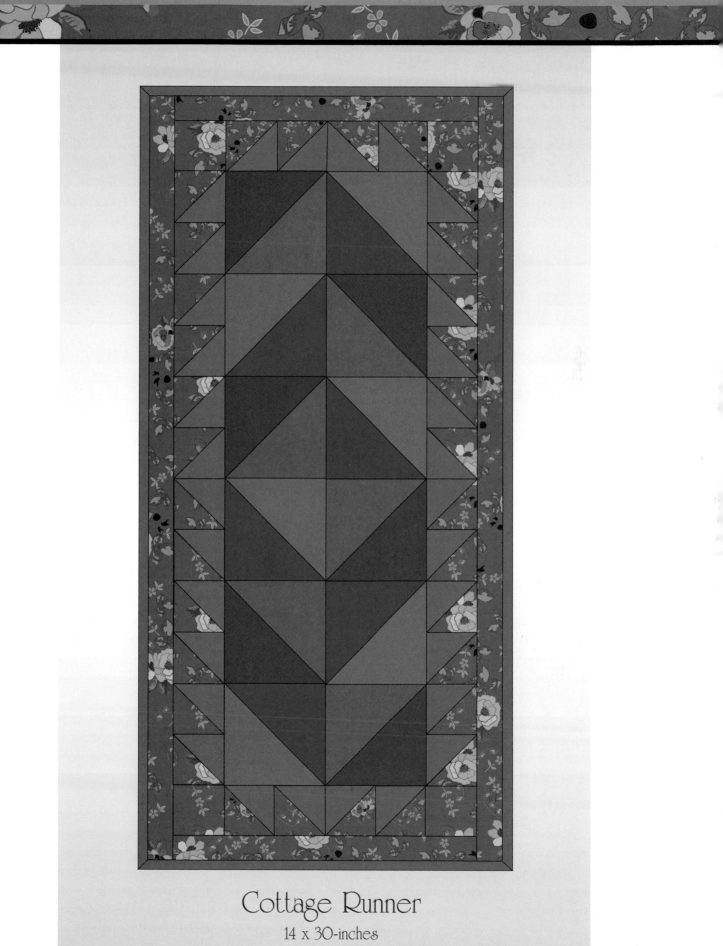

Cottage Runner
14 x 30-inches

Autumn Night

20 x 38-inches

Fabrics & Supplies

1/4 yard **GREEN PRINT**
for nine-patch blocks

1/4 yard **BLACK/GOLD FLORAL**
for nine-patch blocks

1/4 yard **BEIGE PRINT**
for alternate blocks

1/4 yard **BLACK PRINT** for inner border

3/8 yard **GOLD PRINT** for outer border

3/8 yard **BLACK PRINT** for binding

3/4 yards for backing

quilt batting, at least 26 x 42-inches

*Before beginning this project,
read through **Getting Started** on page 181.*

Runner Center

Makes 5 nine-patch blocks

Cutting

From **BEIGE PRINT**:
• Cut 1, 6-1/2 x 44-inch strip. From strip cut:
  5, 6-1/2-inch alternate blocks

From **GREEN PRINT**:
• Cut 3, 2-1/2 x 44-inch strips

From **BLACK/GOLD FLORAL**:
• Cut 3, 2-1/2 x 44-inch strips

Piecing
Refer to arrows on diagrams for pressing.

Step 1 With right sides together and long edges aligned, sew 2-1/2 x 44-inch **GREEN** strips to both side edges of a 2-1/2 x 44-inch **BLACK/GOLD FLORAL** strip. Press referring to ***Hints and Helps for Pressing Strip Sets*** on page 187. Crosscut the strip set into segments.

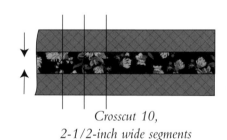

*Crosscut 10,
2-1/2-inch wide segments*

Step 2 With right sides together and long edges aligned, sew 2-1/2 x 44-inch **BLACK/GOLD FLORAL** strips to both side edges of a 2-1/2 x 44-inch **GREEN** strip; press. Crosscut the strip set into segments.

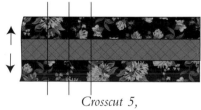

*Crosscut 5,
2-1/2-inch wide segments*

Step 3 Sew the Step 1 segments to the top/bottom edges of the Step 2 segments; press. <u>At this point each nine-patch block should measure 6-1/2-inches square.</u>

Make 5

Runner Center Assembly

Step 1 Sew together the alternate blocks and nine-patch blocks in pairs; press.

Step 2 Sew the pairs together to make the runner center; press. <u>At this point the runner center should measure 12-1/2 x 30-1/2-inches.</u>

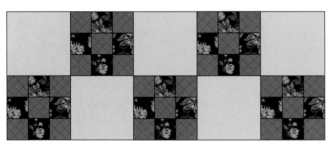

Borders

*Note: Yardage given allows for border strips to be cut on the crosswise grain. Diagonally piece the strips as needed, referring to **Diagonal Piecing** on page 189. Read through **Border** instructions on page 187 for instructions on adding borders.*

Cutting

From **BLACK PRINT**:
• Cut 3, 1-1/2 x 44-inch inner border strips

From **GOLD PRINT**:
• Cut 3, 3-1/2 x 44-inch outer border strips

Attaching Borders

Press seam allowances toward borders just added.

Step 1 Attach 1-1/2-inch wide **BLACK PRINT** inner border strips.

Step 2 Attach 3-1/2-inch wide **GOLD PRINT** outer border strips.

Putting It All Together

Trim backing and batting so they are 6-inches larger than the runner top. Refer to *Finishing the Quilt* on page 189 for complete instructions.

Quilting Suggestions:

• **BEIGE** alternate squares **TB52 – 5-1/2" Oak Leaf**

• Nine-patch blocks – in-the-ditch

• **BLACK** inner border – in-the-ditch

• **GOLD** outer border **TB115 – 2-1/2" Leaf Wave**

TB52-5-1/2" Oak Leaf

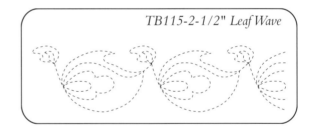

TB115-2-1/2" Leaf Wave

THIMBLEBERRIES® *quilt stencils by Quilting Creations International are available at your local quilt shop or visit www.quiltingcreations.com.*

Binding

Cutting

From **BLACK PRINT**:
• Cut 4, 2-3/4 x 44-inch strips.

Sew binding to runner using a 3/8-inch seam allowance. This measurement will produce a 1/2-inch wide finished double binding. Refer to **Binding** and **Diagonal Piecing** on page 189 for complete instructions.

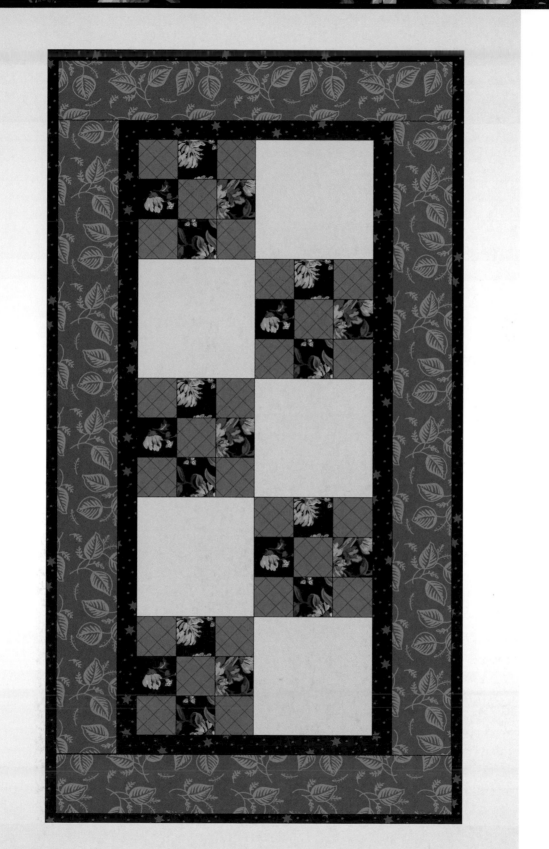

Autumn Night Runner
20 x 38-inches

Picket Post

22 x 48-inches

Fabrics & Supplies

1/3 yard	**LIGHT GOLD PRINT** for quilt center
1/4 yard	**BEIGE PRINT** for quilt center
1/4 yard	**BLUE PRINT** for quilt center
7/8 yard	**RED PRINT** for border

(4) 4-1/2-inch squares of
5 COORDINATING PRINTS
for a total of 20 yo-yo flowers

1/8 yard	**GREEN PRINT** for stems
3/8 yard	**GREEN PRINT** for binding

1-1/2 yards for backing

quilt batting, at least 28 x 54-inches

template material for yo-yos
(posterboard, manila folder)

*Before beginning this project,
read through **Getting Started** on page 181.*

Quilt Center

Cutting

From **LIGHT GOLD PRINT**:
- Cut 2, 4-1/2 x 44-inch strips. From strips cut:
  5, 4-1/2 x 10-1/2-inch rectangles
  1, 2-1/2 x 10-1/2-inch rectangle

From **BEIGE PRINT**:
- Cut 1, 4-1/2 x 44-inch strip. From strip cut:
  2, 4-1/2 x 10-1/2-inch rectangles

- Cut 1, 2-1/2 x 44-inch strip. From strip cut:
  3, 2-1/2 x 10-1/2-inch rectangles

From **BLUE PRINT**:
- Cut 1, 4-1/2 x 44-inch strip. From strip cut:
  7, 4-1/2-inch squares

- Cut 1, 2-1/2 x 44-inch strip. From strip cut:
  4, 2-1/2-inch squares

Piecing

Step 1 With right sides together, position a 4-1/2-inch **BLUE** square on the right corner of a 4-1/2 x 10-1/2-inch **LIGHT GOLD** rectangle. Draw a diagonal line on the square and stitch on the line. Trim seam allowance to 1/4-inch; press.

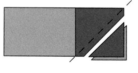 

Make 2 using
LIGHT GOLD

Repeat this step reversing the direction of the drawn line.

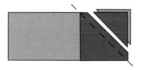 

Make 3 using
LIGHT GOLD

Step 2 With right sides together, position a 4-1/2-inch **BLUE** square on the left corner of a 4-1/2 x 10-1/2-inch **BEIGE** rectangle. Draw a diagonal line on the square; stitch on the line, trim, and press.

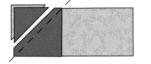

Make 2 using **BEIGE**

Step 3 With right sides together, position a 2-1/2-inch **BLUE** square on the left corner of a 2-1/2 x 10-1/2-inch **LIGHT GOLD** rectangle. Draw a diagonal line on the square, stitch on the line, trim, and press.

Make 1 using
LIGHT GOLD

Step 4 With right sides together, position a 2-1/2-inch **BLUE** square on the right corner of a 2-1/2 x 10-1/2-inch **BEIGE** rectangle. Draw a diagonal line on the square, stitch on the line, trim, and press.

Make 2 using **BEIGE**

Repeat this step reversing the direction of the drawn line.

Make 1 using **BEIGE**

Step 5 Sew the Step 1 - 4 units together, press. <u>At this point the runner center should measure 10-1/2 x 36-1/2-inches.</u>

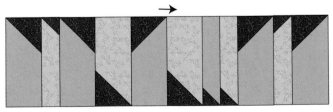

Make 1

Border

Note: *Yardage given allows for border strips to be cut on crosswise grain. Read through* ***Border*** *instructions on page 187 for general instructions on adding borders.*

The yo-yo flowers and stems will be added after the runner is quilted.

Cutting

From **RED PRINT**:

• Cut 4, 6-1/2 x 44-inch border strips

Attaching Border

Step 1 Attach 6-1/2-inch wide **RED** border strips to long side edges of quilt.

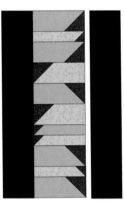

Step 2 Attach 6-1/2-inch wide **RED** border strips to short side edges of quilt.

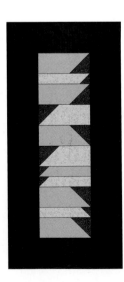

Putting It All Together

Trim backing and batting so they are 6-inches larger than the runner top. Refer to *Finishing the Quilt* on page 189 for complete instructions.

Quilting Suggestions:

- 4" wide fence sections - 1/2" wide channel stitch
- 2" wide fence sections - 1/4" wide channel stitch
- **BLUE** triangles - stipple
- **RED** outer border - **TB37 – 5" Pansy Vine**

TB37-5" Pansy Vine

THIMBLEBERRIES® *quilt stencils by Quilting Creations International are available at your local quilt shop or visit www.quiltingcreations.com.*

Stem Appliqué

Cutting

From **GREEN PRINT**:
- Cut 2, 1-3/8 x 44-inch strips

Appliqué the Stems

Step 1 Fold each 1-3/8-inch wide **GREEN** strip in half lengthwise, wrong sides together; press. To keep raw edges aligned, stitch a scant 1/4-inch away from raw edges. Fold strip in half again so raw edges are hidden by first folded edge; press. At this point the strip should be about 3/8-inch wide.

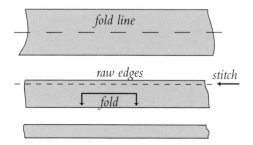

fold line

raw edges   *stitch*

fold

From **PREPARED GREEN** strips:
- Cut 12, 4-1/2-inch long stems
- Cut 8, 2-1/2-inch long stems

Step 2 With raw edges aligned, position prepared stems on the border; pin in place. With matching thread, hand or machine appliqué stems in place. The binding will be stitched over the stem ends.

Yo-Yo Flowers

Step 1 Trace yo-yo pattern (page 22) onto template material; cut out.

Step 2 Using the 3-5/8-inch circle template, trace 20 circles (4 of each color) on the wrong side of the fabric chosen for the yo-yos. Cut on the drawn lines.

Step 3 To make each yo-yo, turn edges of circle under a scant 1/8-inch. Take care to keep seam allowances of each circle the same size. Use one strand of quilting thread to make running stitches close to the fold. Make stitches approximately 1/4-inch long and 1/4-inch apart. If the running stitches are made too close together, it will be difficult to pull up the stitches to make a nice tight hole at the yo-yo center.

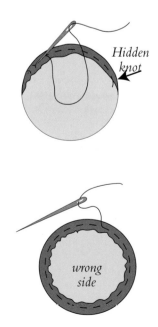

Hidden knot

wrong side

Step 4 To form yo-yo, pull up gathering thread so the circle is gathered on the right side. Pull thread tight; knot and bury the thread in the fold of the yo-yo. The back side of the yo-yo will be flat. <u>At this point the finished yo-yo should measure 1-3/4-inches in diameter.</u>

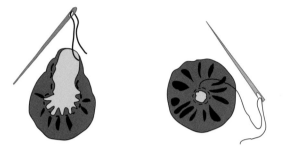

Step 5 Repeat to make the remaining yo-yo flowers. Position the yo-yos on the border so the stem ends are covered. Hand stitch the edges of the yo-yo flowers in place.

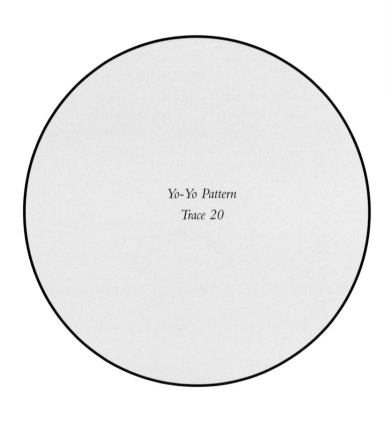

Yo-Yo Pattern
Trace 20

Binding

Cutting

From **GREEN PRINT**:
• Cut 4, 2-3/4 x 44-inch strips.

Sew binding to runner using a 3/8-inch seam allowance. This measurement will produce a 1/2-inch wide finished double binding. Refer to ***Binding*** and ***Diagonal Piecing*** on page 189 for complete instructions.

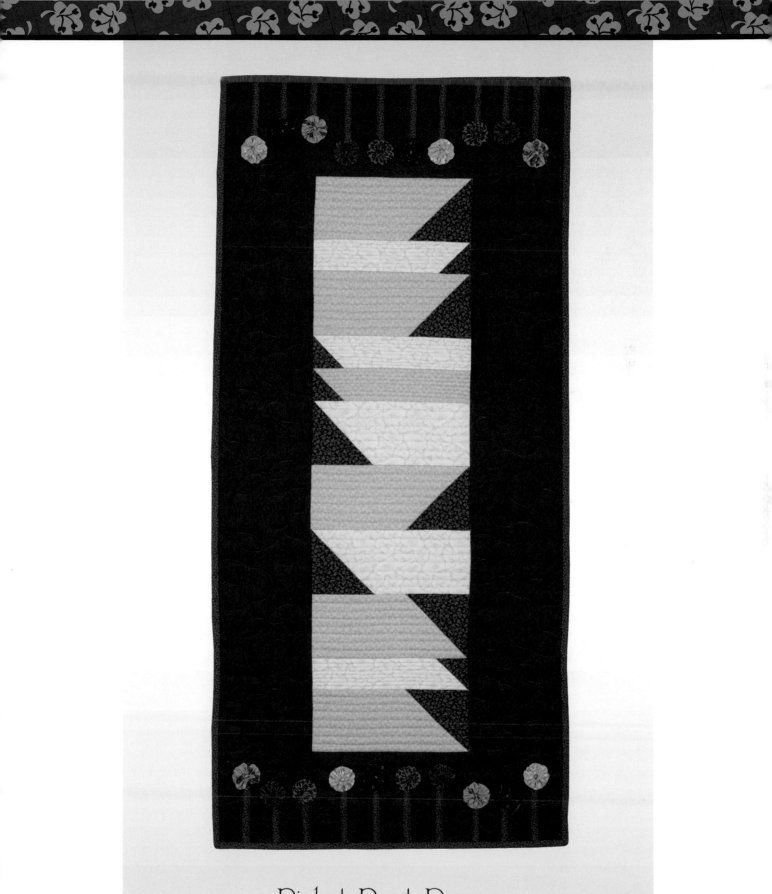

Picket Post Runner

22 x 48-inches

table runners

Button Loop

12-1/2 x 39-inches

Fabrics & Supplies

1/8 yard *each*   **6 COORDINATING PRINTS**
for runner top

3/8 yard   **DARK BLUE PRINT**
for binding, button loops

(3) 14-inch squares backing

(3) 14-inch squares quilt batting

(6) 7/8-inch diameter buttons

temporary basting spray

*Before beginning this project,
read through* **Getting Started** *on page 181.*

Runner Top

Cutting

From *each* of the **6 COORDINATING PRINTS**.
• Cut 1, 2-1/2 x 44-inch strip. From each strip cut:
  3, 2-1/2 x 14-inch strips

Piecing

The 3 blocks will be quilted using the quilt-as-you-go method.

Step 1   Draw vertical lines on the batting squares as a guide to help keep the 2-1/2-inch wide **COORDINATING PRINT** strips straight while they are stitched in place.

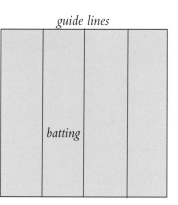

guide lines

batting

Step 2   Lay a 14-inch backing square on the table, face down. Lightly spray temporary fabric adhesive on the backing. With the marked side up, position a batting square on top of the backing; pat in place.

Step 3   Position a 2-1/2 x 14-inch **COORDINATING PRINT** strip, right side up, on the left edge of the batting/backing unit. Now position a second 2-1/2 x 14-inch strip, wrong side up, on top of the first strip. Stitch through all the thicknesses, 1/4-inch from the right aligned raw edges. Fold back the second strip and finger-press or lightly iron.

right side

batting

wrong side

batting

stitch through all layers

Step 4 Continue adding the strips in this manner until 6 strips are added. Be very careful to keep the strips parallel to the edges of the batting. <u>Trim each pieced block to 12-1/2-inches square.</u> Hand baste the edges together to prevent them from rippling when the binding is added.

Button Loops

Cutting

From **DARK BLUE PRINT**:

• Cut 1, 2 x 44-inch strip. From strip cut:
    6, 2 x 6-inch rectangles for button loops

Piecing

Step 1 To make a loop, fold both long edges of a 2 x 6-inch **DARK BLUE** rectangle in to the center of the rectangle; press. Fold in half again to make a strip 1/2 x 6-inches. Edge-stitch close to the folded edges. Make a total of 6 strips.

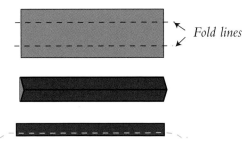

Fold lines

Step 2 Referring to the diagram, fold each strip in half so it lays flat and forms a "triangle" at the top edge; press. Stitch along the bottom edge of the "triangle" to make each button loop.

Stitch

Step 3 With right sides together and raw edges aligned, position each loop along both sides of the center square; pin. The loops should be pointed toward the center of the square at this time. Make sure the buttons will fit through the loops; adjust the loops if needed. Machine baste the loops in place.

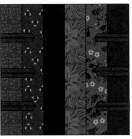

Make 1

Binding

Cutting

From **DARK BLUE PRINT**:

• Cut 4, 2-3/4 x 44-inch strips.

Attach binding to the 3 pieced squares using a 3/8-inch seam allowance. This measurement will produce a 1/2-inch wide finished double binding. Refer to **Binding** and **Diagonal Piecing** on page 189 for complete instructions.

Finishing the Runner

Step 1 Flip the loops back so they point away from the center block; pin in place. Lay the remaining blocks next to the center block. Our blocks are spaced 1/2-inch apart. Position the buttons on the outer blocks aligning them with the button loops. Stitch the buttons in place.

Step 2 Remove the pins from the loops and slip the loops over the buttons. The loops should be held down by the buttons at this time. If you would like, stitch the base of the loops to the binding.

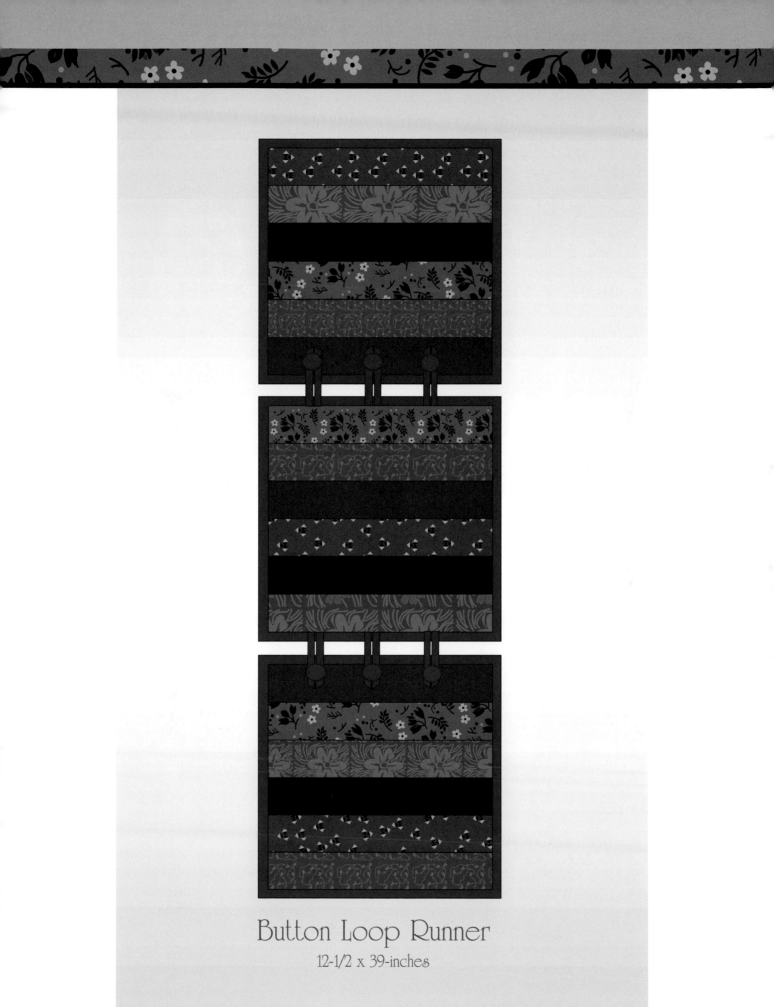

Button Loop Runner

12-1/2 x 39-inches

table runners

Reindeer

24 x 47-inches

Fabrics & Supplies

| 1/8 yard | **6 ASSORTED BEIGE PRINTS** for quilt center |

1/4 yard   **RED PRINT** for inner border

2/3 yard   **GREEN PRINT** for outer border

3/8 yard   **BLACK PRINT** for binding

1-1/2 yards for backing

quilt batting, at least 30 x 53-inches

Appliqué Fabrics & Supplies

1/4 yard   **BLACK PRINT** for reindeer appliqués

1/8 yard   **GOLD PRINT** for star appliqués

paper-backed fusible web

pearl cotton or machine embroidery thread for decorative stitches: black, gold

template material

tear-away fabric stabilizer

*Before beginning this project, read through **Getting Started** on page 181.*

Quilt Center

Cutting

From **6 ASSORTED BEIGE PRINTS**:

• Cut 1, 2-1/2 x 44-inch strip from each fabric

Piecing

Refer to arrows on diagrams for pressing.

With right sides together and long edges aligned, sew the 2-1/2 x 44-inch **BEIGE** strips together. Press referring to *Hints and Helps for Pressing Strip Sets* on page 187. Trim the runner center to 12-1/2 x 35-1/2-inches.

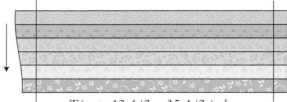

Trim to 12-1/2 x 35-1/2-inches

Paper-Backed Fusible Web Appliqué

Step 1   Make templates using shapes on pages 31–32. Trace shapes on paper side of fusible web.

Step 2   When you are fusing a large shape like the reindeer, fuse just the outer edges of the shape so the center is softer to the touch and it will not look stiff when finished. Cut away fusible web about 3/8-inch inside the shape.

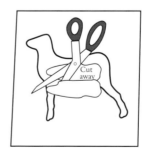
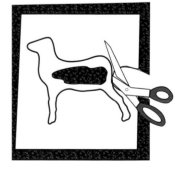

Step 3 Following manufacturer's instructions, fuse shapes to wrong side of fabrics chosen for appliqués. Let fabric cool and cut along traced line. Peel away paper backing from fusible web. Position appliqué shapes on runner center.

Step 4 For machine appliqué, we suggest pinning a square of tear-away stabilizer to backside of runner center so it will lay flat when machine appliqué is complete. Machine blanket stitch around shapes using machine embroidery thread. Our project was blanket stitched by hand with pearl cotton.

Start here → *Blanket Stitch*

Note: To prevent hand blanket stitches from "rolling off" edges of appliqué shapes, take an extra backstitch in the same place as you made the blanket stitch, going around outer curves, corners, and points. For straight edges, taking a backstitch every inch is enough.

Borders

*Note: Yardage given allows for border strips to be cut on the crosswise grain. Diagonally piece the strips as needed, referring to **Diagonal Piecing** on page 189. Read through **Border** instructions on page 187 for instructions on adding borders.*

Cutting

From **RED PRINT**:
• Cut 3, 1-1/2 x 44-inch inner border strips

From **GREEN PRINT**:
• Cut 4, 5-1/2 x 44-inch outer border strips

Attaching Borders

Press seam allowances toward borders just added.

Step 1 Attach 1-1/2-inch wide **RED** inner border strips to long edges first.

Step 2 Attach 5-1/2-inch wide **GREEN** outer border strips to long edges first.

Putting It All Together

Trim backing and batting so they are 6-inches larger than the runner top. Refer to **Finishing the Quilt** on page 189 for complete instructions.

Quilting Suggestions:

- **BEIGE** - stipple around appliqué shapes

- **RED** inner border - in-the-ditch

- **GREEN** outer border
  TB76 - 3-1/2" Holly Chain

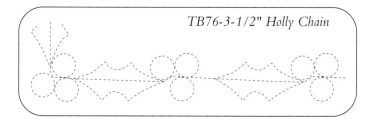

TB76-3-1/2" Holly Chain

THIMBLEBERRIES® *quilt stencils by Quilting Creations International are available at your local quilt shop or visit www.quiltingcreations.com.*

Binding

Cutting

From **BLACK PRINT**:
- Cut 4, 2-3/4 x 44-inch strips.

Sew binding to runner using a 3/8-inch seam allowance. This measurement will produce a 1/2-inch wide finished double binding. Refer to **Binding** and **Diagonal Piecing** on page 189 for complete instructions.

Appliqué Pieces

The appliqué shapes are reversed for tracing purposes. When the appliqué is finished it will appear as in the illustration.

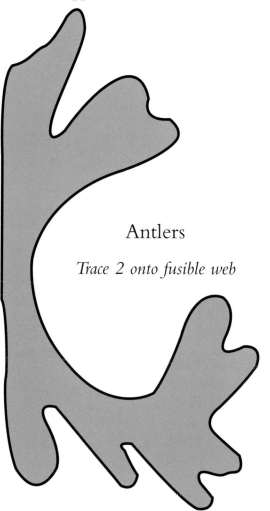

Antlers

Trace 2 onto fusible web

Stars

Trace 6 onto fusible web

Appliqué Pieces

The appliqué shapes are reversed for tracing purposes.
When the appliqué is finished it will appear as in the illustration.

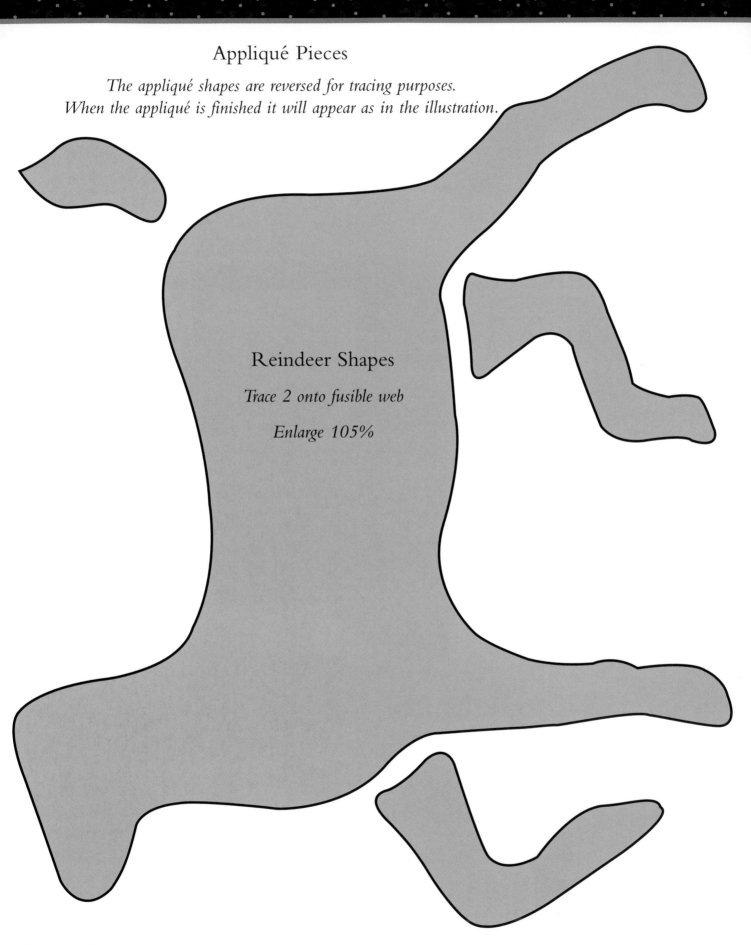

Reindeer Shapes

Trace 2 onto fusible web

Enlarge 105%

Reindeer Runner

24 x 17-inches

Mad for Plaid

55-inches square

Fabrics & Supplies

1-3/8 yards **GREEN PRINT** for blocks, outer border

3/8 yard **GOLD PRINT** for blocks, lattice

7/8 yard **BLUE FLORAL** for blocks

1/4 yard **BEIGE PRINT** for blocks

3/8 yard **ROSE PRINT** for blocks, inner border

5/8 yard **BLUE FLORAL** for binding

3-1/2 yards for backing

quilt batting, at least 61-inches square

*Before beginning project,
read through **Getting Started** on page 181.*

Blocks

Makes 4 blocks

Cutting

From **GREEN PRINT**:
• Cut 6, 2 x 44-inch strips

From **GOLD PRINT**:
• Cut 4, 1-1/2 x 44-inch strips

From **BLUE FLORAL**:
• Cut 1, 7 x 44-inch strip. From strip cut:
    4, 7-inch center squares
• Cut 8, 2-1/2 x 44-inch strips. From strips cut:
    8, 2-1/2 x 19-inch side border strips
    8, 2-1/2 x 15-inch top/bottom border strips

From **BEIGE PRINT**:
• Cut 3, 2-1/2 x 44-inch strips. From strips cut:
    16, 2-1/2 x 4-1/2-inch rectangles
    16, 2-1/2-inch squares

From **ROSE PRINT**:
• Cut 1, 2-1/2 x 44-inch strip. From strip cut:
    16, 2-1/2-inch squares

Piecing

Refer to arrows on diagrams for pressing.

Step 1 Aligning long edges, sew together 3 of the 2 x 44-inch **GREEN** strips and 2 of the 1-1/2 x 22-inch **GOLD** strips. Make 2 strip sets. Press referring to **Hints and Helps for Pressing Strip Sets** on page 187. Cut strip sets into segments.

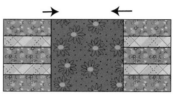

Cut 16, 4-1/2-inch wide segments

Step 2 Sew 2 of the Step 1 segments to side edges of a 7-inch **BLUE FLORAL** center square; press. At this point each unit should measure 7 x 15-inches.

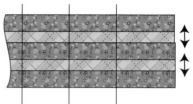

Make 4

Step 3 Aligning long edges, sew together the 2-1/2 x 44-inch **BEIGE** and **ROSE** strips. Press referring to **Hints and Helps for Pressing Strip Sets**. Cut strip set into segments. Referring to diagrams, sew 2-1/2 x 4-1/2-inch **BEIGE** rectangles to the side edge of each segment; press. At this point each corner square should measure 4-1/2-inches square.

Crosscut 16, 2-1/2-inch wide segments   *Make 8*   *Make 8*

Step 4 Sew Step 3 corner squares to both side edges of remaining Step 1 segments; press. At this point each unit should measure 4-1/2 x 15-inches.

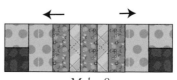

Make 8

Step 5 Sew together the Step 2 and Step 4 units; press. <u>At this point each block should measure 15-inches square.</u>

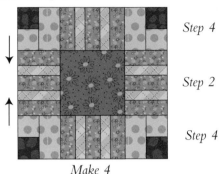

Make 4

Step 6 Sew 2-1/2 x 15-inch **BLUE FLORAL** border strips to top/bottom edges of each block; press. Sew 2-1/2 x 19-inch **BLUE FLORAL** border strips to side edges; press. <u>At this point each block should measure 19-inches square.</u>

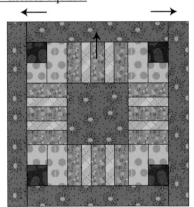

Make 4

Lattice and Borders

Note: Yardage given allows for lattice and border strips to be cut on crosswise grain. Diagonally piece strips as needed referring to **Diagonal Piecing** *instructions on page 189. Read through* **Border** *instructions on page 187 for general instructions on adding borders.*

Cutting

From **GOLD PRINT**:
- Cut 2, 2-1/2 x 44-inch strips. From strips cut:
    - 1, 2-1/2 x 39-1/2-inch lattice strip
    - 2, 2-1/2 x 19-inch lattice strips

From **ROSE PRINT**:
- Cut 4, 2-1/2 x 44-inch inner border strips

From **GREEN PRINT**:
- Cut 5, 6-1/2 x 44-inch outer border strips

Attaching Lattice Strips and Borders

Step 1 Sew blocks to both side edges of the 2-1/2 x 19-inch **GOLD** lattice strips; press. Make 2 block rows. Sew the block rows to the top/bottom edges of the 2-1/2 x 39-1/2-inch **GOLD** lattice strips; press. <u>At this point the quilt center should measure 43-1/2-inches square.</u>

Step 2 Attach 2-1/2-inch wide **ROSE** inner border strips.

Step 3 Attach 6-1/2-inch wide **GREEN** outer border strips.

Putting It All Together

Cut 3-1/2 yard length of backing fabric in half crosswise to make 2, 1-3/4 yard lengths. Refer to *Finishing the Quilt* on page 189 for complete instructions.

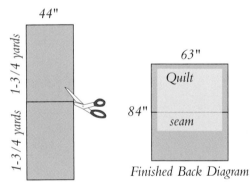

Finished Back Diagram

Quilting Suggestions:

- **BLUE FLORAL** center squares – **TB84 – 5-1/2" Heart Swirl** & stipple behind stencil to fill up the square.

- In-the-ditch around squares, rectangles, & borders

- **BLUE** block borders – **TB30 – 1-1/2" Beadwork**

- **GOLD** lattice & **ROSE** inner border – **TB94 – 2-1/2" M-Border**

- **GREEN** outer border – **TB44 – 5-1/2" Star Vine Border**

THIMBLEBERRIES® *quilt stencils by Quilting Creations International are available at your local quilt shop or visit www.quiltingcreations.com.*

Binding

Cutting

From **BLUE FLORAL**:
- Cut 6, 2-3/4 x 44-inch strips

Sew binding to quilt using a 3/8-inch seam allowance. This measurement will produce a 1/2-inch wide finished double binding. Refer to *Binding* and *Diagonal Piecing* on page 189 for complete instructions.

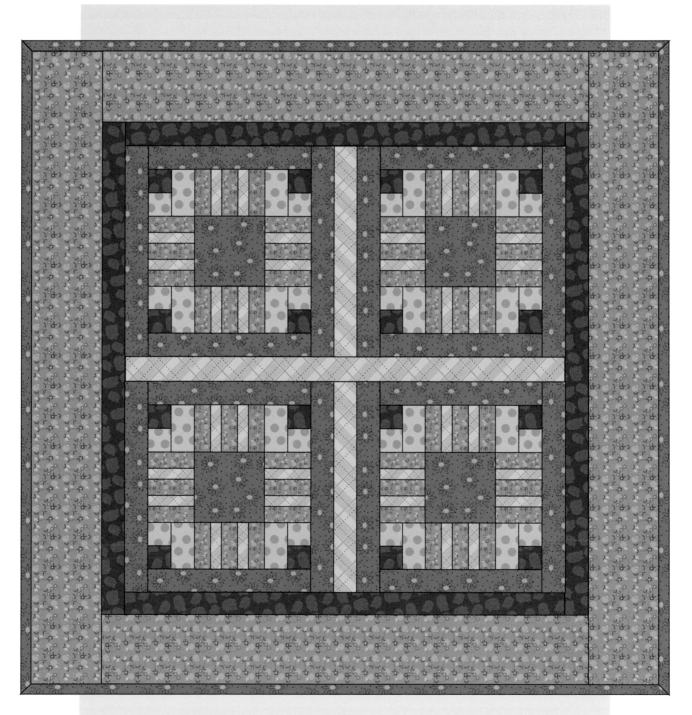

Mad for Plaid Table Topper

55-inches square

table toppers

Caterpillar Cabin Square

42-inches square

Fabrics & Supplies

1/4 yard	*each* of **7 ORANGE PRINTS** for quilt top
1/4 yard	*each* of **7 GREEN PRINTS** for quilt top
6-1/2-inch square	**BLACK/ORANGE PRINT** for center square
1/2 yard	**BLACK PRINT** for binding

1-1/4 yards for backing -

> *Note:* Use a multi-color backing so your quilting/stitching thread will not be noticeable on the backing when you quilt-as-you-go.

quilt batting, at least 45-inches square

temporary fabric spray adhesive

spray water bottle, chenille brush

black 3/8-inch wide & 5/8-inch wide Chenille-It™ Blooming Bias™ strips (BB117/3 & BB117/5)

> *Before beginning this project, read through **Getting Started** on page 181.*

The caterpillar Cabin Square is made using the traditional Courthouse Steps Log Cabin block - made extra big. To make this project even easier, the instructions show you how to quilt-as-you-go. For a fun, dimensional twist... we stitched chenille strips along the seam lines.

Quilt Top

Cutting

From **BLACK/ORANGE PRINT**:
• Cut 1, 6-1/2-inch square

From *each* of the **7 ORANGE PRINTS**:
• Cut 2, 2-1/2 x 44-inch strips. From strips cut:
  8, 2-1/2 x 10-1/2-inch strips

From *each* of the **7 GREEN PRINTS**:
• Cut 2, 2-1/2 x 44-inch strips. From strips cut:
  8, 2-1/2 x 10-1/2-inch strips

From **BACKING**:
• Cut 1, 44-inch square

Piecing

Chenille strips are layered on each of the seams. Each seam has a 5/8-inch wide chenille strip and a 3/8-inch wide chenille strip.

Step 1 With wrong side up, lay the 44-inch **BACKING** square on a protected flat surface. Lightly spray fabric adhesive on the wrong side of the **BACKING** (follow manufacturer's instructions). Lay the **BATTING** square on top of the **BACKING**, smooth out from center to edges; pat in place.

Step 2 The center square <u>must be</u> placed exactly at the center of the batting/backing unit. Position the 6-1/2-inch **BLACK/ORANGE** center square, right side up, on the batting/backing square; pin in place.

Step 3 With right sides together, position 2-1/2-inch wide **ORANGE** strips on the side edges of the center square. Using a 1/4-inch seam allowance, stitch through the 2 layers of fabric, batting, and backing. Finger-press the **ORANGE** strips open. Using a scissors, trim the strips even with the edges of the center square.

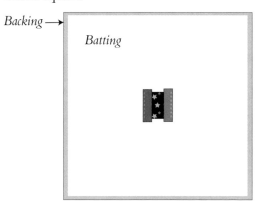

Backing →

Batting

Step 4 Position a 5/8-inch wide and a 3/8-inch wide chenille strip on each seam. Stitch through the center of the strips. Spray water on the chenille strips. Using the chenille brush, gently brush the edges of the strips to roughen them up.

Position chenille strips on seams and sew in place

Step 5 With right sides together, position 2-1/2-inch wide **GREEN** strips on the top and bottom edges of the unit. Stitch through all the layers. Finger-press the **GREEN** strips open. Trim the strips even with the edges of the **ORANGE** strips. Stitch layered chenille strips in place; spray and brush.

Step 6 At this point, randomly sew the 2-1/2 x 10-1/2-inch **ORANGE** strips together end-to-end. Also, randomly sew the 2-1/2 x 10-1/2-inch **GREEN** strips together end-to-end.

Step 7 Referring to the illustration on page 41, sew pieced 2-1/2-inch wide **ORANGE** strips to the side edges of the unit; finger-press and trim. Stitch layered chenille strips in place; spray and brush.

Step 8 Sew pieced 2-1/2-inch wide **GREEN** strips to the top/bottom edges of the unit; finger-press and trim. Stitch layered chenille strips in place; spray and brush.

Step 9 Continue this process until you have 9 pieced strips (and chenille strips) on each side of the center square. Finger-press and trim the ends of the strips even to keep the quilt top square. At this point the quilt top should measure 42-1/2-inches square.

Binding
Cutting

From **BLACK PRINT**:
• Cut 5, 2-3/4 x 44-inch strips

Sew binding to quilt using a 3/8-inch seam allowance. This measurement will produce a 1/2-inch wide finished double binding. Refer to **Binding** and **Diagonal Piecing** on page 189 for complete instructions.

Caterpillar Cabin Square

42-inches square

Easy Breezy

49-inches square

Fabrics & Supplies

2/3 yard	**BEIGE FLORAL** for center square, corner squares
1/4 yard	**GREEN PRINT** for inner border
1/4 yard	**GOLD PRINT #1** for one middle border
1/4 yard	**GOLD PRINT #2** for one middle border
1/4 yard	**ROSE PRINT #1** for one middle border
1/4 yard	**ROSE PRINT #2** for one middle border
1-1/2 yards	**LARGE FLORAL** for outer border
1/2 yard	**GREEN PRINT** for binding

3 yards for backing

quilt batting, at least 55-inches square

*Before beginning this project,
read through **Getting Started** on page 181.*

Quilt Center

*Note: Yardage given allows for border strips to be cut on crosswise grain. Diagonally piece strips as needed, referring to **Diagonal Piecing** on page 189.*

Cutting

From **BEIGE FLORAL**:
- Cut 1, 21-1/2-inch square
- Cut 4, 4-1/2-inch squares

From **GREEN PRINT**:
- Cut 3, 1-1/2 x 44-inch strips. From strips cut:
    - 2, 1-1/2 x 31-1/2-inch strips
    - 2, 1-1/2 x 21-1/2-inch strips
    - 4, 1-1/2 x 4-1/2-inch strips

From **GOLD PRINT #1** and **GOLD PRINT #2**:
- Cut 1, 4-1/2 x 21-1/2-inch strip from each

From **ROSE PRINT #1** and **ROSE PRINT #2**:
- Cut 1, 4-1/2 x 21-1/2-inch strip from each

Piecing

Refer to arrows on diagrams for pressing.

Step 1 Sew 1-1/2 x 21-1/2-inch **GREEN** strips to top/bottom edges of the 21-1/2-inch **BEIGE FLORAL** square; press. Sew 4-1/2 x 21-1/2-inch **GOLD #1** and **GOLD #2** strips to top/bottom edges of this unit; press.

Step 2 Sew 1-1/2 x 31-1/2-inch **GREEN** strips to both side edges of the quilt center; press.

Step 3 Sew 1-1/2 x 4-1/2-inch **GREEN** strips to both ends of the **ROSE #1** and **ROSE #2** strips; press. Sew 4-1/2-inch **BEIGE FLORAL** corner squares to both ends of the strips; press. Sew the strips to both side edges of the quilt center; press. At this point the quilt center should measure 31-1/2-inches square.

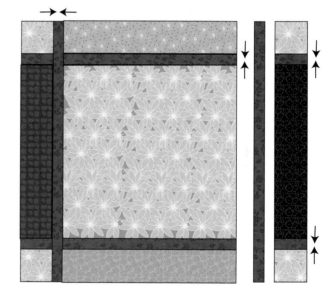

Outer Border

*Note: Yardage given allows for outer border strips to be cut on crosswise grain. Read through **Border** instructions on page 187 for general instructions on adding borders.*

Cutting

From **LARGE FLORAL**:
- Cut 5, 9-1/2 x 44-inch outer border strips

Attaching Outer Border

Attach 9-1/2-inch wide **LARGE FLORAL** outer border strips.

Putting It All Together

Cut 3 yard length of backing fabric in half crosswise to make 2, 1-1/2 yard lengths. Refer to **Finishing the Quilt** on page 189 for complete instructions.

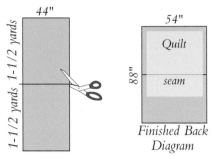

Quilting Suggestions:

- **BEIGE FLORAL** center square –
  (4) **TB86 – 9-1/2" Heart Swirl**

- **GREEN** inner border – in-the-ditch

- **GOLD** and **ROSE** middle borders –
  TB65 – 3-1/2" Nordic Scroll

- **BEIGE** corner squares –
  TB56 – 3-1/2" Ice Crystal

- **LARGE FLORAL** outer border –
  TB43 – 7" Star Vine Border

THIMBLEBERRIES® *quilt stencils by Quilting Creations International are available at your local quilt shop or visit www.quiltingcreations.com.*

Binding

Cutting

From **GREEN PRINT**:

- Cut 5, 2-3/4 x 44-inch strips

Sew binding to quilt using 3/8-inch seam allowance. This measurement will produce a 1/2-inch wide finished double binding. Refer to **Binding** and **Diagonal Piecing** on page 189 for complete instructions.

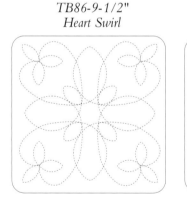

TB86-9-1/2"
Heart Swirl

TB56-3-1/2"
Ice Crystal

TB65-3-1/2" Nordic Scroll

TB43-7" Star Vine Border

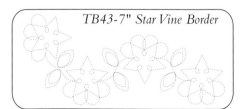

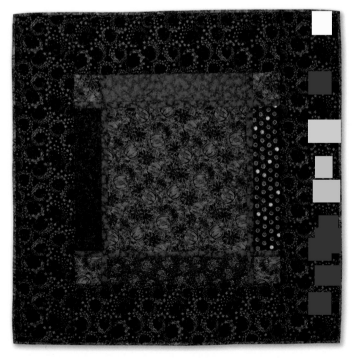

Easy Breezy Color Option
49-inches square

Easy Breezy Table Topper
49-inches square

Zigzag Roundabout

28-inches diameter

Fabrics & Supplies

5/8 yard	**ORANGE PUMPKIN PRINT** for table topper center
3/8 yard	**BLACK PRINT** for border
1/2 yard	**ORANGE PRINT** for border
1/4 yard	**BEIGE PRINT** for border
1/4 yard	**RUST PRINT** for binding

1 yard for backing

quilt batting, at least 34-inches square

*Before beginning project,
read through **Getting Started** on page 181.*

Center Square and Zigzag Border

Cutting

From **ORANGE PUMPKIN PRINT**:
- Cut 1, 20-1/2-inch center square

From **BLACK PRINT**:
- Cut 3, 2-1/2 x 44-inch strips. From strips cut:
  40, 2-1/2-inch squares
- Cut 2, 4-7/8-inch squares.
  Cut the squares diagonally in half
  to make 4 corner triangles.

*4-7/8"
corner triangles*

From **ORANGE PRINT**:
- Cut 6, 2-1/2 x 44-inch strips. From strips cut:
  20, 2-1/2 x 4-1/2-inch rectangles
  40, 2-1/2-inch squares

From **BEIGE PRINT**:
- Cut 3, 2-1/2 x 44-inch strips. From strips cut:
  20, 2-1/2 x 4-1/2-inch rectangles

Piecing

Refer to arrows on diagrams for pressing.

Step 1 With right sides together, position a
2-1/2-inch **BLACK** square on the corner of a
2-1/2 x 4-1/2-inch **ORANGE PRINT** rectangle.
Draw a diagonal line on the square; stitch on the
line. Trim seam allowance to 1/4-inch; press. Repeat
this process at the opposite corner of the rectangle.

Make 20

Step 2 With right sides together, position a
2-1/2-inch **ORANGE PRINT** square on the
corner of a 2-1/2 x 4-1/2-inch **BEIGE** rectangle.
Draw a diagonal line on the square; stitch on
the line, trim, and press. Repeat this process at the
opposite corner of the rectangle.

Make 20

Step 3 Sew Step 1 and Step 2 units together. Press half of
the seam allowances toward the Step 1 units and
press the other half of the seam allowances toward

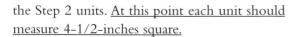

the Step 2 units. At this point each unit should measure 4-1/2-inches square.

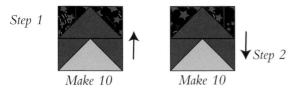

Step 1   *Step 2*

Make 10   Make 10

Step 4   Sew 5 of the units together for each border, paying attention to the direction the seam allowances are pressed. At this point each zigzag border strip should measure 4-1/2 x 20-1/2-inches.

Make 2 top/bottom zigzag borders.
Refer to Step 6 diagram for side zigzag borders.

Step 5   Sew zigzag borders to the top/bottom edges of the 20-1/2-inch **ORANGE PUMPKIN PRINT** center square. Press seam allowances toward the center square.

Step 6   Sew the **BLACK** triangles to the ends of the side zigzag borders; press. Sew the zigzag borders to the side edges of the quilt center; press. At this point the quilt center should measure 28-1/2-inches square.

Make 2 side zigzag borders

Putting It All Together

Trim backing and batting so they are approximately 6-inches larger than quilt top. Refer to *Finishing the Quilt* on page 189 for complete instructions.

Quilting Suggestions:

- **ORANGE PUMPKIN PRINT** center square – diagonal or meander

- **BEIGE** – echo if desired

- **ORANGE PRINT** – echo

- **BLACK** – meander

Binding

Cutting

From **RUST PRINT**:

- Cut 5 to 6, 2-1/2 x 44-inch strips.
  To maintain perfect triangle tips at the outer edges, sew binding to quilt top using a 1/4-inch seam allowance.

Attaching Binding

Step 1   Diagonally piece binding strips referring to *Diagonal Piecing* on page 189. Fold strip in half lengthwise, wrong sides together; press. Unfold and trim one end at a 45° angle. Turn under edge 3/8-inch; press. Refold strip.

Fold Line

Step 2   With raw edges of the binding and quilt top even, stitch with a 1/4-inch seam allowance starting 2-inches from an angled end.

Step 3   Miter the binding at the corners. As you approach a corner (45° angle) of the quilt top, stop sewing 1/4-inch from the corner point. Clip threads and remove quilt top from under presser foot. Flip binding strip up and away from the corner of the quilt top, then fold binding down even with raw edge of the quilt top. Start sewing at upper edge. Miter the (8) 45° angle corners in this manner.

Stop 1/4" from corner point
1/4"

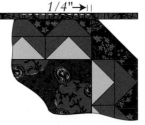

Stop 1/4" from corner point
1/4"

Step 4 Turn the folded edge of the binding over the raw edges and to the back of the quilt top so the stitching line does not show. Corners will naturally turn with very little effort. Pin as needed to create a nice mitered corner on the back as well as on the front. Slip-stitch binding to backside of quilt top by hand.

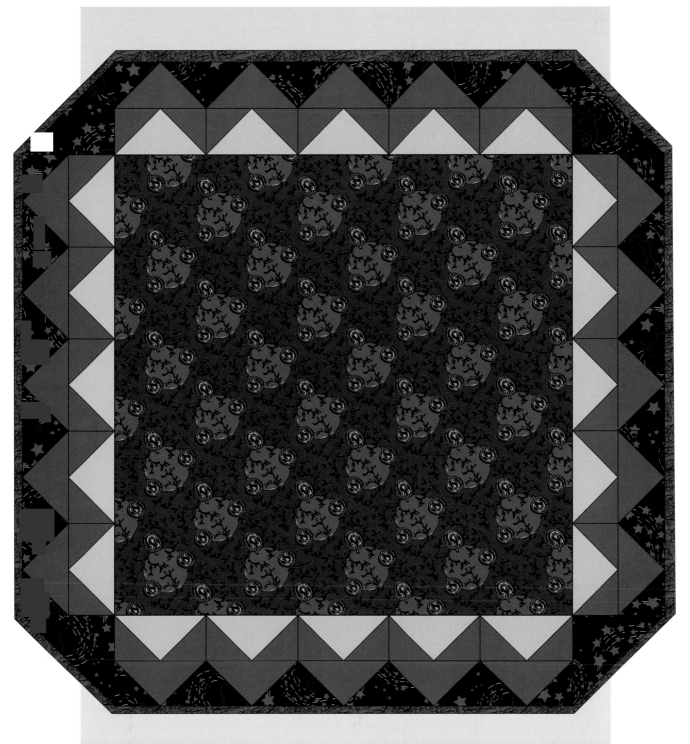

Zigzag Roundabout Table Topper

28-inches diameter

Love Triangle

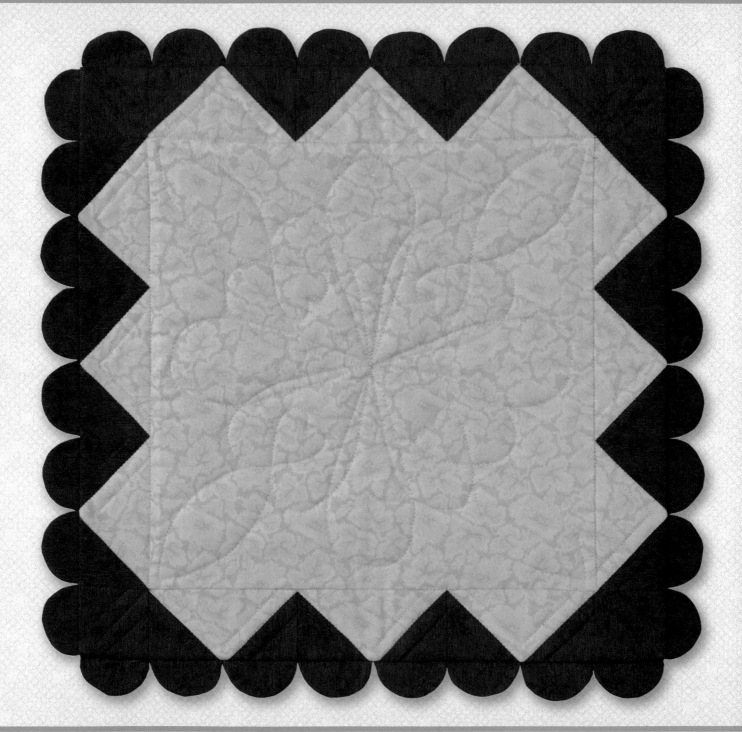

20-inches square

Fabrics & Supplies

7/8 yard **RED PRINT** for hearts, facing, backing

3/8 yard **BEIGE PRINT** for quilt top

quilt batting, at least 22-inches square

Sulky® Flying Colors Thread for quilting
(733-1082 Ecru & 733-1181 Rust)

*Before beginning this project, read through **Getting Started** on page 181.*

Quilt Center

Cutting

From **RED PRINT**:
- Cut 2, 2-1/2 x 44-inch strips. From strips cut:
  28, 2-1/2-inch squares

From **BEIGE PRINT**:
- Cut 1, 12-1/2 x 44-inch strip. From strip cut:
  1, 12-1/2-inch center square
  12, 2-1/2 x 4-1/2-inch rectangles

Piecing

Refer to arrows on diagrams for pressing.

Step 1 With right sides together, position a 2-1/2-inch **RED** square on the corner of a 2-1/2 x 4-1/2-inch **BEIGE** rectangle. Draw a diagonal line on the square; stitch on the line. Trim seam allowance to 1/4-inch; press. Repeat this process at the opposite corner of the rectangle.

Make 12

Step 2 Sew together 3 of the Step 1 units; press. Make 4 of the 3-piece units. Sew 2 of the 3-piece units to the top/bottom edges of the 12-1/2-inch **BEIGE** center square. Press seam allowances toward the square.

Make 4

Step 3 Sew 2-1/2-inch **RED** squares to the ends of both of the remaining 3-piece units; press. Sew the units to side edges of square unit; press. <u>At this point the quilt center should measure 16-1/2-inches square.</u> The heart border will be added after the project is quilted.

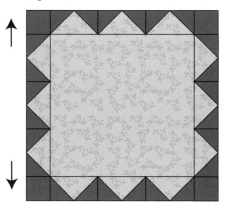

Putting It All Together and Heart Border

Cutting

From **RED PRINT**:
- Cut 1, 22 x 44-inch strip. From strip cut:
    - 1, 22-inch backing square
    - 8, 2 x 22-inch strips for hearts
    - 2, 1-3/4 x 18-inch facing strips
- Cut 1, 1-3/4 x 44-inch strip. From strip cut:
    - 2, 1-3/4 x 18-inch facing strips

Quilt the Quilt Top

Step 1 Mark the quilt top for quilting. Layer the 22-inch backing, batting, and quilt top (facing up). Baste the layers together; quilt as desired.

Quilting Suggestions:

- **BEIGE** center square –
  TB83 – 11-1/2" Heart Loop

TB83-11-1/2" Heart Loop

- Stitch in-the-ditch around the center square & triangles
- Echo quilt in the triangle units
- **RED** corner squares – stitch diagonally to define heart edges

THIMBLEBERRIES® *quilt stencils by Quilting Creations International are available at your local quilt shop or visit www.quiltingcreations.com.*

Step 2 Refer to ***Finishing the Quilt*** on page 189 for complete instructions.

Heart Border

Step 1 Make a template using the Heart Scallop Pattern.

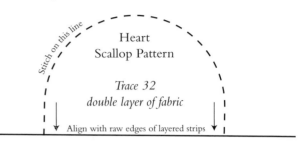

Step 2 With right sides together, layer the 2 x 22-inch **RED** strips in pairs. Press together but do not sew.

Step 3 With a pencil, trace the template on the layered strips, aligning the straight edge of the template with the raw edge of the layered strips, leaving 1/2-inch between each shape for seam allowances. Trace the heart scallop 32 times. Pin the layers together to secure them for sewing.

Trace 32 heart scallops on layered strips

Step 4 Using very short stitches, machine stitch the layered **RED** strips together <u>on the drawn curved lines.</u> Leave the bottom straight edge open for turning. Cut out the scallops allowing a 1/8-inch seam allowance. Turn the scallops right side out; press. Make 32 **RED** scallops.

Step 5 Referring to diagram, pin and hand baste 8 **RED** heart scallops to the top/bottom edges of the quilt top. Do not overlap the heart scallops. <u>The heart scallops at the ends should be 1/4-inch from the quilt top raw edges to allow for seam allowances.</u>

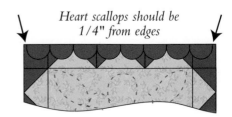

Heart scallops should be 1/4" from edges

Step 6 With wrong sides together, fold each 1-3/4 x 18-inch **RED** facing strip in half lengthwise; press. With raw edges aligned, position 2 of the folded strips on top of the heart scallops (top/bottom edges of the quilt top). Stitch in place with a 1/4-inch seam allowance. Trim away excess facing even with the quilt top edges.

Stitch 1/4" seam allowance and trim excess facing even with quilt top edges.

Step 7 Fold the facing to the back of the quilt top; hand stitch in place. <u>At this point the heart scallops will lay out flat.</u>

Step 8 Pin and hand baste 8 heart scallops to the side edges of the quilt top. Do not overlap the heart scallops. <u>The end heart scallops should go right to the edges of the quilt top - there is no need to allow for a seam allowance.</u>

Heart scallops should go right to the edges

Step 9 Position the remaining prepared **RED** facing strips on top of the heart scallops (side edges of the quilt top). Stitch in place with a 1/4-inch seam allowance. **DO NOT** trim the facing ends. Turn the excess facing ends under and fold the strip to the back of the quilt top so there will not be any raw edges showing; hand stitch in place. <u>At this point the heart scallops will lay out flat.</u>

Stitch 1/4" seam allowance

Love Triangle Table Square
20-inches square

Holiday Spirit

40-inches square

Fabrics & Supplies

5/8 yard	**BEIGE PRINT** for quilt center
1/3 yard	**RED PRINT** for inner and middle borders
1-1/8 yards	**DARK GREEN PRINT** for middle border, outer border
1/2 yard	**LIGHT GREEN PRINT** for binding cut on the bias

1-1/4 yards for backing

quilt batting, at least 44-inches square

paper for scallop edge templates

Before beginning this project,
*read through **Getting Started** on page 181.*

Borders

Note: *Yardage given allows for border strips to be cut on crosswise grain. Read through **Border** instructions on page 187 for general instructions on adding borders.*

Cutting

From **BEIGE PRINT**:
• Cut 1, 18-1/2-inch center square

From **RED PRINT**:
• Cut 6, 1-1/2 x 44-inch border strips

From **DARK GREEN PRINT**:
• Cut 3, 1-1/2 x 44-inch middle border strips
• Cut 4, 8-1/2 x 44-inch outer border strips

Attaching Borders

Press seam allowances toward borders just added.

Step 1 Attach 1-1/2-inch wide **RED** inner border strips to 18-1/2-inch **BEIGE** center square.

Step 2 Attach 1-1/2-inch wide **GREEN** middle border strips.

Step 3 Attach 1-1/2-inch wide **RED** middle border strips.

Step 4 Attach 8-1/2-inch wide **GREEN** outer border strips.

Putting It All Together

Step 1 To mark the scallop edges, use the templates provided. Trace and cut the templates out of paper which you can pin through. Lay the templates against the **RED** middle border, pin to keep from shifting and mark the scallop lines onto the **GREEN** outer border. **Do not cut along these lines until after the project is quilted.** Mark all 4 sides.

Step 2 Mark the quilt top for quilting. Layer the backing, batting, and quilt top. Baste the 3 layers together and quilt.

Quilting Suggestions:

• **BEIGE** center square – stitch (4) **TB54 – 7-1/2" Pine Tree** & stipple behind stencil

• Quilt the 3 narrow borders as 1 border – **TB31 – 3" Blossom Swirl**

• **GREEN** outer border – small meander

TB54-7-1/2" Pine Tree

THIMBLEBERRIES® *quilt stencils by Quilting Creations International are available at your local quilt shop or visit www.quiltingcreations.com.*

Step 3 When quilting is complete, baste the layers together a scant 1/4-inch <u>inside</u> the drawn scallop edge. This hand basting keeps the layers from shifting and prevents puckers from forming when adding the binding. Trim excess backing and batting even with the drawn scallop edge of the table topper.

Binding

Cutting

From **LIGHT GREEN PRINT**:
• Cut enough 2-1/4-inch wide *bias* strips to make a strip 170-inches long.

Sew binding to quilt using a 1/4-inch seam allowance. Refer to **Binding** and **Diagonal Piecing** on page 189 for complete instructions.

Attaching Binding to Scallop Edges

This is a gentle scallop and should be fairly easy to bind if you follow these suggestions.

- Always use **bias** binding for a nice, smooth binding around curves. Pin the raw edge of the bias binding to the edge of the quilt top. Do not pin the entire binding on, just a few inches ahead as you stitch the binding in place. As you stitch, gently ease a little extra binding onto the curved edge. This will prevent the scalloped edges from "cupping" when finished. This happens when the binding is accidentally stretched as it is sewn on.

- At the inside point of the scallops, with your needle in the down position, raise your presser foot so you can maneuver the quilt and binding. Realign the raw edges, lower the presser foot, and continue stitching. With the tip of a pin or needle, push the edge of the

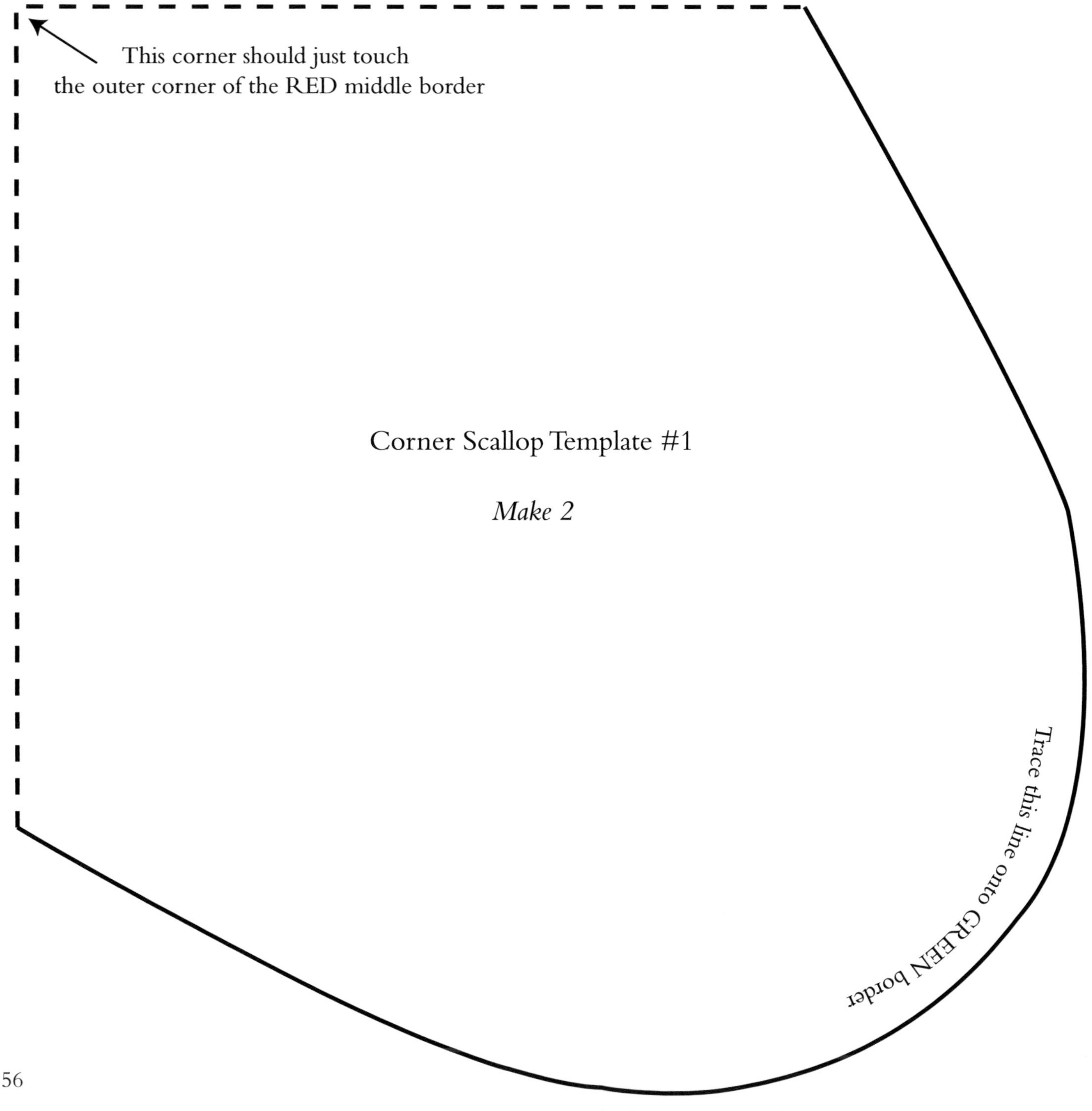

This corner should just touch the outer corner of the RED middle border

Corner Scallop Template #1

Make 2

Trace this line onto GREEN border

binding, making sure it continues to meet the edge of the quilt. This will create a small amount of fullness in the binding at the pivot points, which will be concealed when the folded edge of the binding is hand stitched to the back of the quilt.

- Trim the end of the binding so it can be tucked inside of the beginning binding about 1/2-inch.

- Turn the binding to the back of the quilt and hand stitch the folded edge in place.

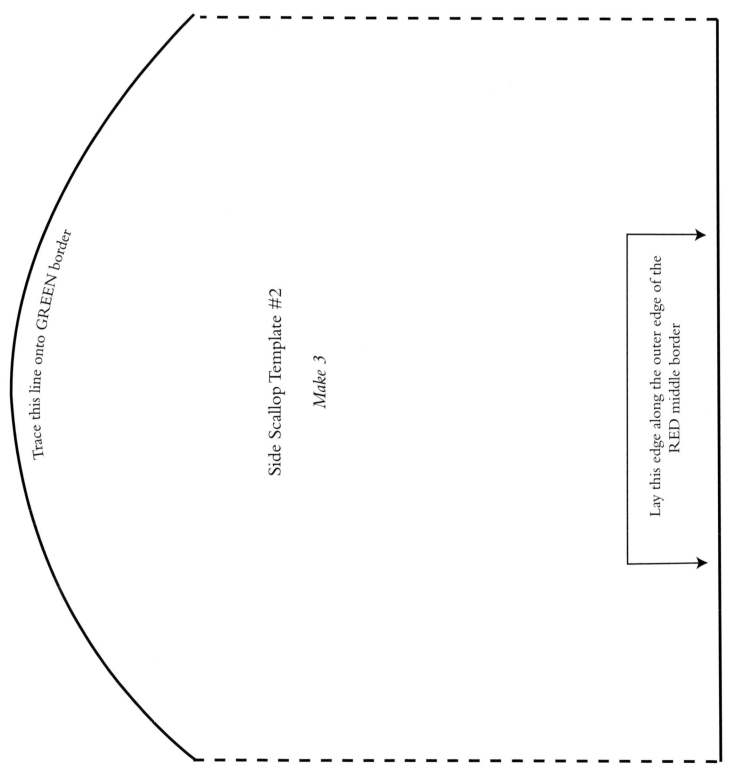

Trace this line onto GREEN border

Side Scallop Template #2

Make 3

Lay this edge along the outer edge of the RED middle border

Pumpkin Hill House

60 x 64-inches

Fabrics & Supplies

3/4 yard	**BROWN PRINT** for house block, hourglass corner squares
5/8 yard	**BLACK PRINT #1** for house block, pumpkin blocks, hourglass corner squares
3/4 yard	**BEIGE PRINT #1** for house block, dogtooth border
1/4 yard	**RUST PUMPKIN PRINT** for house block
3/4 yard	**BEIGE PRINT #2** for house block, leaf blocks, pumpkin blocks, pieced border
1 yard	**GREEN PRINT** for inner border, middle/dogtooth border
1/2 yard	**BLACK PRINT #2** for pieced border
1/3 yard	**RED/MULTI-COLOR PRINT** for leaf blocks
1/4 yard	**ORANGE PRINT** for pumpkin blocks
1/8 yard	**PLUM PRINT** for spacer rectangles
1/8 yard	**GOLD PRINT** for spacer rectangles
1/8 yard	**BROWN/BLACK PRINT** for spacer rectangles
1-1/2 yards	**HALLOWEEN SIGNATURE PRINT** for outer border
5/8 yard	**GREEN PRINT** for binding

3-3/4 yards for backing

quilt batting, at least 66 x 70-inches

pearl cotton or embroidery floss
for decorative stitches: black

*Before beginning this project,
read through **Getting Started** on page 181.*

House Block

Cutting

From **BROWN PRINT**:
- Cut 1, 8-7/8 x 44-inch strip. From strip cut:
    1, 8-7/8-inch square
    1, 6-7/8-inch square
    1, 6-1/2-inch square
- Cut 1, 4-1/2 x 44-inch strip. From strip cut:
    2, 4-1/2 x 10-1/2-inch rectangles
    1, 2-1/2 x 4-1/2-inch rectangle

From **BLACK PRINT #1**:
- Cut 1, 4-1/2 x 44-inch strip. From strip cut:
    1, 4-1/2 x 14-1/2-inch rectangle
    1, 4-1/2 x 8-1/2-inch rectangle
    2, 4-1/2-inch squares
- Cut 1, 2-1/2 x 10-1/2-inch rectangle

From **BEIGE PRINT #1**:
- Cut 1, 8-7/8 x 44-inch strip. From strip cut:
    1, 8-7/8-inch square
    1, 2-1/2 x 14-1/2-inch rectangle

From **RUST PUMPKIN PRINT**:
- Cut 1, 6-7/8 x 44-inch strip. From strip cut:
    1, 6-7/8-inch square
    1, 6-1/2-inch square
    From remainder of strip cut:
    2, 2-1/2 x 28-inch strips. From strips cut:
    1, 2-1/2 x 10-1/2-inch rectangle
    2, 2-1/2 x 6-1/2-inch rectangles
    1, 2-1/2 x 4-1/2-inch rectangle
    2, 2-1/2-inch squares

From **BEIGE PRINT #2**:
- Cut 1, 6-1/2-inch square
- Cut 1, 4-1/2-inch square

Piecing

Refer to arrows on diagrams for pressing.

Step 1 With right sides together, layer the 8-7/8-inch **BROWN** and **BEIGE #1** squares. Press together, but do not sew. Cut the layered square in half diagonally to make 2 sets of triangles. Stitch 1/4-inch from the diagonal edge of each pair of triangles; press. With right sides together, position a 4-1/2-inch **BLACK #1** square on the **BROWN** corner of each triangle-pieced square. Draw a diagonal line on the **BLACK #1** square; stitch on the line. Trim seam allowance to 1/4-inch; press. Sew the 2 units together; press. <u>At this point the roof unit should measure 8-1/2 x 16-1/2-inches.</u>

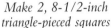

Make 2, 8-1/2-inch triangle-pieced squares

Make 2   *Make 1*

Step 2 With right sides together, layer the 6-7/8-inch **RUST PUMPKIN PRINT** and **BROWN** squares. Cut the layered square in half diagonally to make 1 triangle set. Stitch 1/4-inch from the diagonal edge of the triangle set; press.

Make 1, 6-1/2-inch triangle-pieced square

Step 3 Sew the 4-1/2-inch **BEIGE #2** square to the top edge of the 2-1/2 x 4-1/2-inch **RUST PUMPKIN PRINT** rectangle; press. Sew the Step 2 triangle-pieced square to the right edge of the window unit and sew the 6-1/2-inch **RUST PUMPKIN PRINT** square to the left edge of the unit; press. <u>At this point the unit should measure 6-1/2 x 16-1/2-inches.</u>

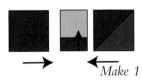

Make 1

Step 4 Referring to the house block assembly diagram on page 61, sew the Step 1 roof unit to the top edge of the Step 3 unit; press. <u>At this point the unit should measure 14-1/2 x 16-1/2-inches.</u>

Step 5 Aligning long raw edges, sew together the 2-1/2 x 14-1/2-inch **BEIGE #1** rectangle and the 4-1/2 x 14-1/2-inch **BLACK #1** rectangle; press. With right sides together, position the 6-1/2-inch **BROWN** square on

the corner of the chimney unit. Draw a diagonal line on the square; stitch, trim, and press. <u>At this point the chimney unit should measure 6-1/2 x 14-1/2-inches.</u> Referring to the house block assembly diagram on page 61, sew the chimney unit to the right edge of the Step 4 unit; press. <u>At this point the unit should measure 14-1/2 x 22-1/2-inches.</u>

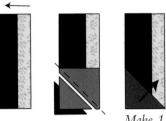

Make 1

Step 6 Sew the 2-1/2 x 6-1/2-inch **RUST PUMPKIN PRINT** rectangles to both side edges of the 6-1/2-inch **BEIGE #2** square to make a window unit; press. With right sides together, position 2-1/2-inch **RUST PUMPKIN PRINT** squares on both ends of the 2-1/2 x 10-1/2-inch **BLACK #1** rectangle. Draw a diagonal line on the squares; stitch, trim, and press to make a window box unit. Sew the 2-1/2 x 10-1/2-inch **RUST PUMPKIN PRINT** rectangle to the bottom edge of the unit; press. Sew the window unit to the top edge of the window box unit; press. <u>At this point the unit should measure 10-1/2-inches square.</u>

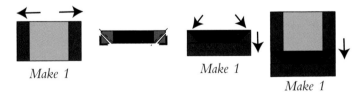

Make 1   *Make 1*   *Make 1*

Step 7 Sew the 2-1/2 x 4-1/2-inch **BROWN** rectangle to the top edge of the 4-1/2 x 8-1/2-inch **BLACK #1** rectangle; press. Sew the 4-1/2 x 10-1/2-inch **BROWN** rectangles to the side edges of the unit; press. <u>At this point the door unit should measure 10-1/2 x 12-1/2-inches.</u>

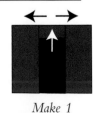

Make 1

Step 8 Sew the Step 6 window unit to the left edge of the Step 7 door unit; press. <u>At this point the unit should measure 10-1/2 x 22-1/2-inches.</u>

Step 9 Referring to the house block assembly diagram, sew the units together to make the house block; press. <u>At this point the house block should measure 22-1/2 x 24-1/2-inches.</u> The window panes can be outline stitched at this time.

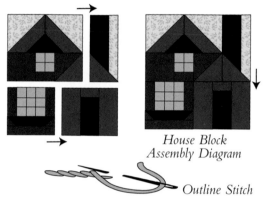

House Block Assembly Diagram

Outline Stitch

Inner Border and Pieced Border

Note: Yardage given allows for border strips to be cut on crosswise grain. Diagonally piece strips as needed referring to **Diagonal Piecing** *instructions page 189. Read through* **Border** *instructions on page 187 for general instructions on adding borders.*

Cutting

From **GREEN PRINT**:
• Cut 4, 1-1/2 x 44-inch inner border strips

From **BLACK PRINT #2**:
• Cut 1, 6-7/8 x 44-inch strip. From strip cut:
    1, 6-7/8-inch square.
    From remainder of strip cut:
    1, 6-1/2 x 32-inch strip. From strip cut:
    5, 6-1/2-inch squares
• Cut 1, 6-1/2 x 44-inch strip. From strip cut:
    5, 6-1/2-inch squares

From **BEIGE PRINT #2**:
• Cut 1, 6-7/8 x 44-inch strip. From strip cut:
    1, 6-7/8-inch square.
    From remainder of strip cut:
    1, 6-1/2 x 32-inch strip. From strip cut:
    2, 6-1/2 x 12-1/2-inch rectangles
• Cut 1, 6-1/2 x 44-inch strip. From strip cut:
    2, 6-1/2 x 12-1/2-inch rectangles

Piecing

Refer to arrows on diagrams for pressing.

Step 1 Attach 1-1/2-inch wide **GREEN** inner border strips. <u>At this point the quilt center should measure 24-1/2 x 26-1/2-inches.</u>

Trim away excess fabric   *Trim away excess fabric*

Step 2 With right sides together, layer the 6-7/8-inch **BLACK #2** and **BEIGE #2** squares. Press together, but do not sew. Cut the layered square in half diagonally to make 2 sets of triangles. Stitch 1/4-inch from the diagonal edge of each pair of triangles; press.

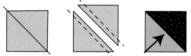

Make 2, 6-1/2-inch triangle-pieced squares

Step 3 With right sides together, position a 6-1/2-inch **BLACK #2** square on the corner of a 6-1/2 x 12-1/2-inch **BEIGE #2** rectangle. Draw a diagonal line on the square; stitch, trim, and press. Repeat this process at the opposite corner of the rectangle.

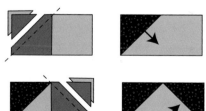

Make 4

Step 4 Sew together 2 of the Step 3 units; press. <u>At this point the unit should measure 6-1/2 x 24-1/2-inches.</u> Sew the unit to the top edge of the quilt center; press.

Make 1 for top edge

Step 5 Sew a Step 2 triangle-pieced square to the left edge of a Step 3 unit and sew a 6-1/2-inch **BLACK #2** square to the right edge; press. Make 1 unit for the left side. Sew the remaining Step 2 triangle-pieced square to the right edge of a Step 3 unit and sew a 6-1/2-inch **BLACK #2** square to the left edge; press. Make 1 unit for the right side. At this point each unit should measure 6-1/2 x 24-1/2-inches. Set the units aside.

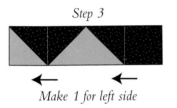

Step 3

Step 3

Make 1 for left side

Make 1 for right side

Leaf Blocks

Makes 3 blocks

Cutting

From **RED/MULTI-COLOR PRINT**:

• Cut 1, 2-7/8 x 44-inch strip. From strip cut:
    2, 2-7/8-inch squares
    3, 1 x 5-inch stem rectangles

• Cut 2, 2-1/2 x 44-inch strips. From strips cut:
    9, 2-1/2 x 4-1/2-inch rectangles
    3, 2-1/2-inch squares

From **BEIGE PRINT #2**:

• Cut 1, 2-7/8 x 44-inch strip. From strip cut:
    2, 2-7/8-inch squares
    3, 2-5/8-inch squares. Cut squares in half diagonally to make 6 triangles for stem units
    9, 2-1/2-inch squares

 2-5/8-inch

Piecing

Refer to arrows on diagrams for pressing.

Step 1 With right sides together, position a 2-1/2-inch **BEIGE #2** square on the corner of a 2-1/2 x 4-1/2-inch **RED/MULTI-COLOR** rectangle. Draw a diagonal line on the square; stitch on line, trim, and press.

Make 6 units for right side. Sew the right side units together in pairs; press. Make 3 units for left side.

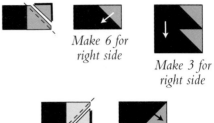

Make 6 for right side

Make 3 for right side

Make 3 for left side

Step 2 With right sides together, layer 2-7/8-inch **BEIGE #2** and **RED/MULTI-COLOR** squares in pairs. Cut the layered squares in half diagonally to make 3 triangle sets. Stitch 1/4-inch from diagonal edge of each triangle set; press.

 *Make 3, 2-1/2-inch triangle-pieced squares*

Step 3 Sew together a triangle-pieced square and a 2-1/2-inch **RED/MULTI-COLOR** square; press. Sew a Step 1 right side unit to the bottom edge; press.

Step 1 right side unit

Make 3 for right side

Step 4 To make a stem unit, center a **BEIGE #2** triangle on a 1 x 5-inch **RED/MULTI-COLOR** rectangle; stitch a 1/4-inch seam. Center another **BEIGE #2** triangle on the opposite edge of the strip; stitch and press. Trim stem unit so it measures 2-1/2-inches square. Sew stem units to bottom edge of Step 1 left side units; press.

Trim

Trim *Make 3 stem units*

Make 3 for left side

Step 1 left side unit

Step 5 Sew the Step 4 units to the left edge of the Step 3 units; press. <u>At this point each leaf block should measure 6-1/2-inches square.</u>

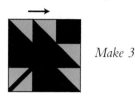

Make 3

Pumpkin Blocks

Makes 4 blocks

Cutting

From **ORANGE PRINT**:
- Cut 2, 3-1/2 x 44-inch strips. From strips cut:
  8, 3-1/2 x 6-1/2-inch rectangles

From **BEIGE PRINT #2**:
- Cut 2, 1-1/2 x 44-inch strips. From strips cut:
  12, 1-1/2 x 3-1/2-inch rectangles
  4, 1-1/2 x 2-1/2-inch rectangles
  16, 1-1/2-inch squares

From **BLACK PRINT #1**:
- Cut 1, 1-1/2 x 44-inch strip. From strip cut:
  20, 1-1/2-inch squares

Piecing

Refer to arrows on diagrams for pressing.

Step 1 With right sides together, position a 1-1/2-inch **BLACK #1** square on the corner of a 1-1/2 x 3-1/2-inch **BEIGE #2** rectangle. Draw a diagonal line on the square; stitch on line. Trim seam allowance to 1/4-inch; press. Make 8 units. Sew the units together in pairs; press.

Make 8   *Make 4*

Step 2 Sew together a 1-1/2 x 3-1/2-inch **BEIGE #2** rectangle, a 1-1/2-inch **BLACK #1** square, and a 1-1/2 x 2-1/2-inch **BEIGE #2** rectangle; press. Make 4 units. Sew the units to the bottom edge of the Step 1 units; press.

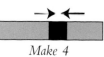

Make 4

Make 4

Step 3 With right sides together, position a 1-1/2-inch **BLACK #1** square on the upper right corner of a 3-1/2 x 6-1/2-inch **ORANGE** rectangle. Draw a diagonal line on the square; stitch on line, trim, and press. Repeat this process at the upper left and lower left corners of the rectangle using 1-1/2-inch **BEIGE #2** squares.

Make 4

Step 4 With right sides together, position a 1-1/2-inch **BLACK #1** square on the upper left corner of a 3-1/2 x 6-1/2-inch **ORANGE** rectangle. Draw a diagonal line on the square; stitch on line, trim, and press. Repeat this process at the upper right and lower right corners of the rectangle using 1-1/2-inch **BEIGE #2** squares.

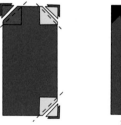

Make 4

Step 5 Sew together the Step 3 and Step 4 units in pairs; press. Sew the Step 2 units to the top edge of these units; press. <u>At this point each pumpkin block should measure 6-1/2 x 8-1/2-inches.</u>

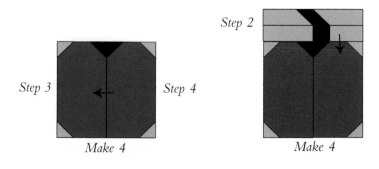

Step 2

Step 3   *Step 4*

Make 4   *Make 4*

Spacer Rectangles and Pieced Border

Cutting

From **PLUM PRINT**:

- Cut 1, 2-1/2 x 44-inch strip. From strip cut:
  2, 2-1/2 x 4-1/2-inch rectangles
  3, 2-1/2 x 3-1/2-inch rectangles

From **GOLD PRINT**:

- Cut 1, 2-1/2 x 44-inch strip. From strip cut:
  2, 2-1/2 x 4-1/2-inch rectangles
  2, 2-1/2 x 3-1/2-inch rectangles

From **BROWN/BLACK PRINT**:

- Cut 1, 2-1/2 x 44-inch strip. From strip cut:
  2, 2-1/2 x 4-1/2-inch rectangles
  1, 2-1/2 x 3-1/2-inch rectangle

Piecing

Refer to arrows on diagrams for pressing.

Step 1 Sew together a 2-1/2 x 3-1/2-inch **PLUM** and **GOLD** rectangle; press. Sew a leaf block to the top edge and a pumpkin block to the bottom edge; press. <u>At this point the left side unit should measure 6-1/2 x 16-1/2-inches.</u>

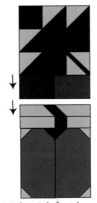

Make 1 left side unit

Step 2 Sew together a 2-1/2 x 3-1/2-inch **PLUM** and **GOLD** rectangle; press. Sew a leaf block and a pumpkin block to the top edge; press. <u>At this point the right side unit should measure 6-1/2 x 16-1/2-inches.</u>

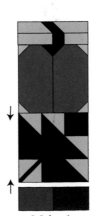

Make 1 right side unit

Step 3 Sew together a 2-1/2 x 3-1/2-inch **PLUM** and **BROWN/BLACK** rectangle; press. Sew a leaf block to the bottom edge; press. Sew together a 2-1/2 x 4-1/2-inch **PLUM** and **GOLD** rectangle; press. Sew this unit to the right edge of the leaf block; press. <u>At this point the unit should measure 8-1/2-inches square.</u>

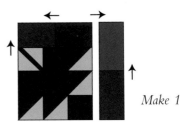

Make 1

Step 4 Sew together a 2-1/2 x 4-1/2-inch **BROWN/BLACK** and **PLUM** rectangle; press. Sew a pumpkin block to the top edge; press. Sew together a 2-1/2 x 4-1/2-inch **GOLD** and **BROWN/BLACK** rectangle; press. Sew to the right edge of the pumpkin block; press. Sew a pumpkin block to the right edge; press. <u>At this point the unit should measure 8-1/2 x 16-1/2-inches.</u>

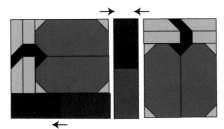

Make 1

Step 5 Sew together the Step 3 and Step 4 units; press. <u>At this point the lower unit should measure 8-1/2 x 24-1/2-inches.</u> Sew the unit to the bottom edge of the house unit; press.

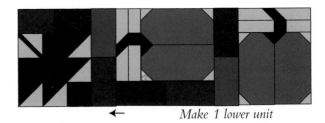

Make 1 lower unit

Step 6 For the left side pieced border, sew together the left side unit (Step 1) and the left prepared pieced border (page 62); press. <u>At this point the unit should measure</u>

6-1/2 x 40-1/2-inches. Sew the unit to the left edge of quilt center; press.

Step 7 For the right side pieced border, sew together the right side unit (Step 2) and the right prepared pieced border (page 62); press. At this point the unit should measure 6-1/2 x 40-1/2-inches. Sew the unit to the right edge of quilt center; press. At this point the quilt center should measure 36-1/2 x 40-1/2-inches.

Quilt Center

Middle Border and Dogtooth Border

Note: Yardage given allows for border strips to be cut on crosswise grain. Diagonally piece strips as needed referring to **Diagonal Piecing** *instructions page 189. Read through* **Border** *instructions on page 187 for general instructions on adding borders.*

Cutting

From **GREEN PRINT**:
• Cut 5, 2-1/2 x 44-inch middle border strips
• Cut 5 more 2-1/2 x 44-inch strips. From strips cut: 42, 2-1/2 x 4-1/2-inch rectangles

From **BEIGE PRINT #1**:
• Cut 6, 2-1/2 x 44-inch strips. From strips cut: 88, 2-1/2-inch squares

Attach Middle Border and Dogtooth Border

Piecing

Refer to arrows on diagrams for pressing.

Step 1 Attach 2-1/2-inch wide **GREEN** middle border strips. At this point the quilt center should measure 40-1/2 x 44-1/2-inches.

Step 2 With right sides together, position a 2-1/2-inch **BEIGE #1** square on the corner of a 2-1/2 x 4-1/2-inch **GREEN** rectangle. Draw a diagonal line on the square; stitch, trim, and press. Repeat this process at the opposite corner of the rectangle.

Make 42

Step 3 For the top/bottom dogtooth borders, sew together 10 of the Step 2 units; press. Make 2 dogtooth borders. At this point each border should measure 2-1/2 x 40-1/2-inches. Sew the dogtooth borders to the top/bottom edges of the quilt center; press.

Make 2 for top/bottom borders

Step 4 For the side dogtooth borders, sew together 11 of the Step 2 units; press. Make 2 dogtooth borders. Sew the 2-1/2-inch **BEIGE #1** squares to both ends of the dogtooth borders. At this point each border should measure 2-1/2 x 48-1/2-inches. Sew the dogtooth borders to the side edges of the quilt center; press. At this point the quilt center should measure 44-1/2 x 48-1/2-inches.

Outer Border and Corner Squares

Note: Yardage given allows for the **HALLOWEEN SIGNATURE PRINT** *outer border strips to be cut on the crosswise grain (diagonally piece as needed) or the lengthwise grain (a couple extra inches are allowed for trimming). Read through* **Border** *instructions on page 187 for general instructions on adding borders.*

Cutting

From **HALLOWEEN SIGNATURE PRINT**:

• Cut 4, 8-1/2 x 51-inch outer border strips
   (cut on lengthwise grain)

OR

• Cut 5, 8-1/2 x 44-inch outer border strips
   (cut on crosswise grain)

From **BLACK PRINT #1**:

• Cut 1, 9-1/4 x 44-inch strip. From strip cut:
   2, 9-1/4-inch squares

From **BROWN PRINT**:

• Cut 1, 9-1/4 x 44-inch strip. From strip cut:
   2, 9-1/4-inch squares

Attach Border

Step 1 Attach top/bottom 8-1/2-inch wide
HALLOWEEN SIGNATURE PRINT
border strips.

Step 2 To make hourglass corner squares, with right
sides together, layer the 9-1/4-inch **BROWN**
and **BLACK #1** squares in pairs; press. Cut
the layered squares diagonally into quarters to
make 8 sets of triangles. Stitch along the same
bias edge of each set of triangles being careful
not to stretch the triangles; press. Sew triangle
units together in pairs; press. At this point
each hourglass corner square should measure
8-1/2-inches square.

Bias edges

*Make 8
triangle units*

*Make 4
hourglass
corner units*

Step 3 For the side borders, measure the quilt
including the seam allowances, but not the
top/bottom borders. Cut the remaining
8-1/2-inch wide **HALLOWEEN
SIGNATURE PRINT** side border
strips to this length. Sew the hourglass
corner squares to each end of the border
strips; press. Sew the borders to the quilt; press.

Putting It All Together

Cut 3-3/4 yard length of backing fabric in
half crosswise to make 2, 1-7/8 yard lengths. Refer
to *Finishing the Quilt* on page 189 for
complete instructions.

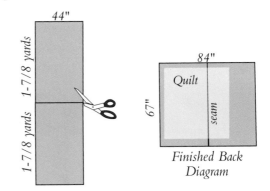

*Finished Back
Diagram*

Quilting Suggestions:

• House – in-the-ditch and echo quilting

• Beige – meander

• Pumpkins – echo quilting

• Outer border – meander

• Spacer rectangles – channel stitching

• Leaves and pieced borders – free hand designs

Binding
Cutting

From **GREEN PRINT**:

• Cut 7, 2-1/2 x 44-inch strips.

Sew binding to the quilt using a 1/4-inch seam
allowance so the hourglass blocks will remain
square. This measurement will produce a 3/8-inch
wide finished double binding. Refer to *Binding*
and *Diagonal Piecing* on page 189 for
complete instructions.

Quilt Cottage

28-inches square

Fabrics & Supplies

1/4 yard	**GOLD PRINT** for stars, windows
1/2 yard	**BEIGE PRINT #1** for background
1/4 yard	**DARK GREEN PRINT** for chimney, checkerboard, door
1/4 yard	**RED PRINT #1** for roof, roof trim
1/8 yard	**MEDIUM GREEN PRINT** for roof trim
1/8 yard	**CHESTNUT PRINT** for house
1/2 yard	**RED PRINT #2** for house, inner & outer border
1/3 yard	**GREEN FLORAL** for fence background, middle border
1/8 yard	**BEIGE PRINT #2** for fence
1/8 yard	**BEIGE PRINT #3** for fence
1/3 yard	**GREEN DIAGONAL PRINT** for binding

1 yard for backing

quilt batting, at least 34-inches square

Before beginning project,
read through **Getting Started** *on page 181.*

Star Blocks

Makes 10 blocks

Cutting

From **GOLD PRINT**:
• Cut 2, 1-1/2 x 44-inch strips. From strips cut:
    10, 1-1/2 x 3-1/2-inch rectangles
    20, 1-1/2-inch squares

From **BEIGE PRINT #1**:
• Cut 3, 1-1/2 x 44-inch strips. From strips cut:
    20, 1-1/2 x 2-1/2-inch rectangles
    40, 1-1/2-inch squares

Piecing

Refer to arrows on diagrams for pressing.

Step 1 With right sides together, position 1-1/2-inch **BEIGE #1** squares on both corners of the 1-1/2 x 3-1/2-inch **GOLD** rectangles. Draw a diagonal line on the squares; stitch on the lines. Trim seam allowances to 1/4-inch; press.

Make 10

Step 2 Position a 1-1/2-inch **GOLD** square on the right corner of a 1-1/2 x 2-1/2-inch **BEIGE #1** rectangle. Draw a diagonal line on the square; stitch on the line, trim, and press. Sew a 1-1/2-inch **BEIGE #1** square to the right edge of the unit; press.

Make 20

Step 3 Sew Step 2 units to the top/bottom edges of the Step 1 units; press. At this point each star block should measure 3-1/2-inches square.

Make 10

Checkerboard

Cutting

From **DARK GREEN PRINT**:
• Cut 2, 1-1/2 x 44-inch strips. From strips cut:
    3, 1-1/2 x 20-inch strips

From **BEIGE PRINT #1**:
• Cut 2, 1-1/2 x 44-inch strips. From strips cut:
    3, 1-1/2 x 20-inch strips

Note: The checkerboard strips are made up of strip sets. Refer to **Hints and Helps for Pressing Strip Sets** *on page 187.*

Piecing

Refer to arrows on diagrams for pressing.

Step 1 With right sides together and long edges aligned, sew 1-1/2 x 20-inch **DARK GREEN** strips to both side edges of a 1-1/2 x 20-inch **BEIGE #1** strip; press. Cut strip set into segments.

Crosscut 12, 1-1/2-inch wide segments

Step 2 Sew 1-1/2 x 20-inch **BEIGE #1** strips to both side edges of a 1-1/2 x 20-inch **DARK GREEN** strip; press. Cut strip set into segments.

Crosscut 10, 1-1/2-inch wide segments

Step 3 Sew 6 of the Step 1 segments and 5 of the Step 2 segments together; press. <u>At this point each checkerboard strip should measure 3-1/2 x 11-1/2-inches.</u>

Make 2

Roof Section

Cutting

From **RED PRINT #1**:
- Cut 1, 4-1/2 x 14-1/2-inch rectangle
- Cut 1, 1-1/2 x 44-inch strip. From strip cut:
    14, 1-1/2-inch squares

From **BEIGE PRINT #1**:
- Cut 2, 4-1/2-inch squares
- Cut 2, 3-1/2-inch squares

From **MEDIUM GREEN PRINT**:
- Cut 1, 1-1/2 x 44-inch strip. From strip cut:
    7, 1-1/2 x 2-1/2-inch rectangles

From **DARK GREEN PRINT**:
- Cut 1, 2-1/2 x 3-1/2-inch rectangle

Piecing

Refer to arrows on diagrams for pressing.

Step 1 With right sides together, position 4-1/2-inch **BEIGE #1** squares on both corners of the 4-1/2 x 14-1/2-inch **RED #1** rectangle. Draw a diagonal line on the squares; stitch on the lines, trim, and press. <u>At this point the roof unit should measure 4-1/2 x 14-1/2-inches.</u>

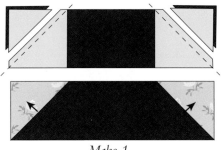

Make 1

Step 2 Position a 1-1/2-inch **RED #1** square on the corner of a 1-1/2 x 2-1/2-inch **MEDIUM GREEN** rectangle. Draw a diagonal line on the square; stitch on the line, trim, and press. Repeat this process at the opposite corner of the rectangle.

Make 7

Step 3 Sew Step 2 units together end to end; press. Sew roof trim strip to bottom edge of roof unit; press. <u>At this point the roof unit should measure 5-1/2 x 14-1/2-inches.</u>

Make 1

Step 4 Sew 3-1/2-inch **BEIGE #1** squares to both sides of the 2-1/2 x 3-1/2-inch **DARK GREEN** rectangle; press. Set chimney unit aside for quilt center assembly.

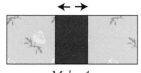

Make 1

House Base

Cutting

From **RED PRINT #2**:
• Cut 1, 1-1/2 x 44-inch strip. From strip cut:
  2, 1-1/2 x 5-1/2-inch rectangles
  4, 1-1/2 x 4-1/2-inch rectangles
  1, 1-1/2 x 2-1/2-inch rectangle

From **GOLD PRINT**:
• Cut 2, 1-1/2 x 4-1/2-inch rectangles

From **CHESTNUT PRINT**:
• Cut 1, 1-1/2 x 44-inch strip. From strip cut:
  4, 1-1/2 x 6-1/2-inch rectangles
  4, 1-1/2 x 3-1/2-inch rectangles

From **DARK GREEN PRINT**:
• Cut 1, 2-1/2 x 4-1/2-inch rectangle
• Cut 1, 1-1/2 x 4-1/2-inch rectangle

Piecing

Refer to arrows on diagrams for pressing.

Step 1 Sew 1-1/2 x 4-1/2-inch **RED #2** rectangles to both side edges of a 1-1/2 x 4-1/2-inch **GOLD** rectangle; press. Sew 1-1/2 x 3-1/2-inch **CHESTNUT** rectangles to the top/bottom edges of this unit; press. Sew 1-1/2 x 6-1/2-inch **CHESTNUT** rectangles to both side edges of this unit; press. At this point the window unit should measure 5-1/2 x 6-1/2-inches.

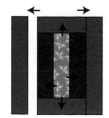

Make 2

Step 2 Sew 1-1/2 x 2-1/2-inch **RED #2** rectangle to the top edge of 2-1/2 x 4-1/2-inch **DARK GREEN** rectangle; press. Sew 1-1/2 x 5-1/2-inch **RED #2** rectangle to both side edges of this unit; press. Sew 1-1/2 x 4-1/2-inch **DARK GREEN** rectangle to bottom edge of the unit; press. At this point the door unit should measure 4-1/2 x 6-1/2-inches.

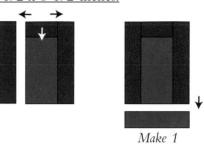

Make 1

Step 3 Sew window units to both side edges of the door unit; press. At this point the house base should measure 6-1/2 x 14-1/2-inches.

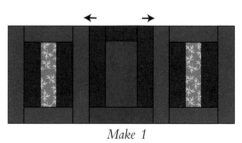

Make 1

Step 4 Sew together roof unit, base unit, and checkerboard strips; press. At this point the house/checkerboard unit should measure 11-1/2 x 20-1/2-inches.

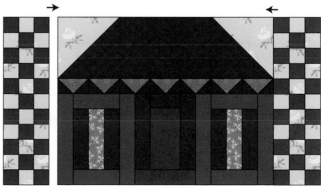

Make 1

Fence Section

Cutting

From **GREEN FLORAL**:

- Cut 1, 1-1/2 x 44-inch strip. From strip cut:
    20, 1-1/2-inch squares

From **BEIGE PRINT #2**:

- Cut 1, 2-1/2 x 44-inch strip. From strip cut:
    6, 2-1/2 x 3-1/2-inch rectangles

From **BEIGE PRINT #3**:

- Cut 1, 1-1/2 x 44-inch strip. From strip cut:
    8, 1-1/2 x 3-1/2-inch rectangles

Piecing

Refer to arrows on diagrams for pressing.

Step 1 Position a 1-1/2-inch **GREEN FLORAL** square on the corner of a 2-1/2 x 3-1/2-inch **BEIGE #2** rectangle. Draw a diagonal line on the square; stitch on the line, trim, and press. Repeat this process at the adjacent corner of the rectangle.

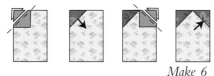

Make 6

Step 2 Position a 1-1/2-inch **GREEN FLORAL** square on the corner of the 1-1/2 x 3-1/2-inch **BEIGE #3** rectangles. Draw a diagonal line on the squares referring to the diagrams for line placement; stitch on the lines, trim, and press.

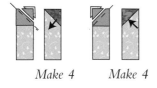

Make 4   *Make 4*

Step 3 Sew the fence pieces together; press. Sew the fence unit to the house/checkerboard unit; press. At this point the house/checkerboard/fence unit should measure 14-1/2 x 20-1/2-inches square.

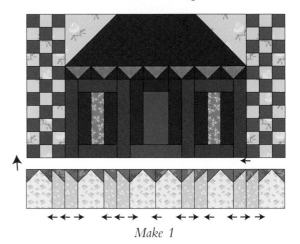

Make 1

Quilt Center

Cutting

From **BEIGE PRINT #1**:

- Cut 1, 2-1/2 x 3-1/2-inch rectangle

Quilt Center Assembly

Refer to arrows on diagrams for pressing.

Step 1 Sew 3 star blocks together to make a star unit; press. Make another star unit. Sew star units to both side edges of the 2-1/2 x 3-1/2-inch **BEIGE #1** rectangle; press. At this point the star unit should measure 3-1/2 x 20-1/2-inches.

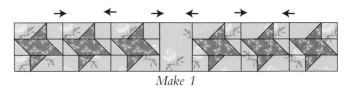

Make 1

Step 2 Sew 2 star blocks together to make a star unit; press. Make another star unit. Sew star units to both side edges of the chimney unit; press. At this point the star/chimney unit should measure 3-1/2 x 20-1/2-inches.

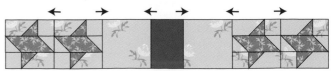

Make 1

Step 3 Referring to the quilt photograph on page 68, sew together the Step 1 and Step 2 units; press. Sew star unit to the top edge of the house unit; press. <u>At this point the quilt center should measure 20-1/2-inches square.</u>

Borders

*Note: Yardage given allows for border strips to be cut on crosswise grain. Read through **Border** instructions on page 187 for general instructions on adding borders.*

Cutting

From **RED PRINT #2**:
• Cut 3, 1 x 44-inch inner border strips
• Cut 4, 2-1/2 x 44-inch outer border strips

From **GREEN FLORAL**:
• Cut 3, 2 x 44-inch middle border strips

Attaching the Borders

Step 1 Attach 1-inch wide **RED #2** inner border strips.

Step 2 Attach 2-inch wide **GREEN FLORAL** middle border strips.

Step 3 Attach 2-1/2-inch wide **RED #2** outer border strips.

Putting It All Together

Trim batting and backing so they are 6-inches larger than quilt top. Refer to *Finishing the Quilt* on page 189 for complete instructions.

Quilting Suggestions:
• **BEIGE** background – stipple
• Roof – crosshatch
• Door, chimney – channel
• House, checkerboard – in-the-ditch
• Fence – channel & in-the-ditch
• Borders – crosshatch

Binding

Cutting

From **GREEN DIAGONAL PRINT**:
• Cut 3, 2-3/4 x 44-inch strips.

Sew binding to quilt using a 3/8-inch seam allowance. This measurement will produce a 1/2-inch wide finished double binding. Refer to *Binding* and *Diagonal Piecing* on page 189 for complete instructions.

Mini Tulip House

21 x 22-inches

Fabrics & Supplies

1/4 yard	**GOLD DOT** for house (roof, door unit)
3/8 yard	**GREEN DIAGONAL PRINT** for house block (chimney, door, window box, roof section), binding
6 x 15-inch piece	**BEIGE FLORAL** for house block (sky)
1/8 yard	**GOLD PRINT** for house block
5 x 8-inch piece	**BEIGE PRINT** for house block (windows)
1/8 yard	**CHESTNUT PRINT** for inner border
1/4 yard	**BLUE PRINT** for middle border, corner squares
1/4 yard	**GOLD/BLUE FLORAL** for outer border

3/4 yard for backing

quilt batting, at least 27 x 30-inches

*Before beginning this project, read through **Getting Started** on page 181.*

Mini Tulip House Block

Makes 1 block

Cutting

From **GOLD DOT**:
- Cut 1, 4-7/8 x 20-inch strip. From the strip cut:
  - 1, 4-7/8-inch square
  - 1, 3-7/8-inch square
  - 1, 3-1/2-inch square
- Cut 1, 2-1/2 x 20-inch strip. From strip cut:
  - 2, 2-1/2 x 5-1/2-inch rectangles
  - 1, 1-1/2 x 2-1/2-inch rectangle

From **GREEN DIAGONAL PRINT**:
- Cut 1, 2-1/2 x 44-inch strip. From strip cut:
  - 1, 2-1/2 x 7-1/2-inch rectangle
  - 1, 2-1/2 x 4-1/2-inch rectangle
  - 2, 2-1/2-inch squares
  - 1, 1-1/2 x 5-1/2-inch rectangle

From **BEIGE FLORAL**:
- Cut 1, 4-7/8-inch square
- Cut 1, 1-1/2 x 7-1/2-inch rectangle

From **GOLD PRINT**:
- Cut 1, 3-7/8 x 44-inch strip. From strip cut:
  - 1, 3-7/8-inch square
  - 1, 3-1/2-inch square
  - 1, 1-1/2 x 5-1/2-inch rectangle
  - 2, 1-1/2 x 3-1/2-inch rectangles
  - 1, 1-1/2 x 2-1/2-inch rectangle
  - 2, 1-1/2-inch squares

From **BEIGE PRINT**:
- Cut 1, 3-1/2-inch square
- Cut 1, 2-1/2-inch square

Piecing

Refer to arrows on diagrams for pressing.

Step 1 With right sides together, layer the 4-7/8-inch **GOLD DOT** and **BEIGE FLORAL** squares. Press together, but do not sew. Cut the layered square in half diagonally to make 2 sets of triangles. Stitch 1/4-inch from the diagonal edge of each pair of triangles; press. With right sides together, position a 2-1/2-inch **GREEN DIAGONAL PRINT** square on the **GOLD DOT** corner of each triangle-pieced square. Draw a diagonal line on the **GREEN DIAGONAL PRINT** square; stitch on the line. Trim seam allowance to 1/4-inch; press. Sew the 2 units together; press. <u>At this point the roof unit should measure 4-1/2 x 8-1/2-inches.</u>

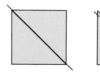
Make 2, 4-1/2-inch triangle-pieced squares

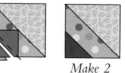
Make 2

Make 1

Step 2 With right sides together, layer the 3-7/8-inch **GOLD PRINT** and **GOLD DOT** squares. Cut the layered square in half diagonally to make 1 triangle set. Stitch 1/4-inch from the diagonal edge of the triangle set; press.

Make 1, 3-1/2-inch triangle-pieced square

Step 3 Sew the 2-1/2-inch **BEIGE PRINT** square to the top edge of the 1-1/2 x 2-1/2-inch **GOLD PRINT** rectangle; press. Sew the Step 2 triangle-pieced square to the right edge of the window unit and sew the 3-1/2-inch **GOLD PRINT** square to the left edge of the unit; press. <u>At this point the unit should measure 3-1/2 x 8-1/2-inches.</u>

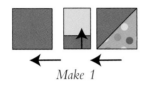

Make 1

Step 4 Referring to the house block assembly diagram, sew the Step 1 roof unit to the top edge of the Step 3 unit; press the seam allowances toward the roof. <u>At this point the unit should measure 7-1/2 x 8-1/2-inches.</u>

Step 5 Aligning long raw edges, sew together the 1-1/2 x 7-1/2-inch **BEIGE FLORAL** rectangle and the 2-1/2 x 7-1/2-inch **GREEN DIAGONAL PRINT** rectangle; press. With right sides together, position the 3-1/2-inch **GOLD DOT** square on the corner of the chimney unit. Draw a diagonal line on the square; stitch on the line, trim, and press. <u>At this point the chimney unit should measure 3-1/2 x 7-1/2-inches.</u> Sew the chimney unit to the right edge of the Step 4 unit; press. <u>At this point the unit should measure 7-1/2 x 11-1/2-inches.</u>

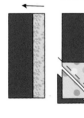 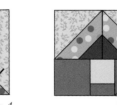 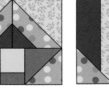

Make 1   *Make 1*

Step 6 Sew the 1-1/2 x 3-1/2-inch **GOLD PRINT** rectangles to both side edges of the 3-1/2-inch **BEIGE PRINT** square to make a window unit; press. With right sides together, position 1-1/2-inch **GOLD PRINT** squares on both ends of the 1-1/2 x 5-1/2-inch **GREEN DIAGONAL PRINT** rectangle. Draw a diagonal line on the squares; stitch, trim, and press to make a window box unit. Sew the

1-1/2 x 5-1/2-inch **GOLD PRINT** rectangle to the bottom edge of the unit; press. Sew the window unit to the top edge of the window box unit. <u>At this point the unit should measure 5-1/2-inches square.</u>

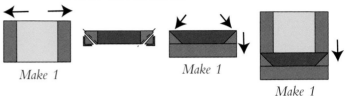

Make 1   *Make 1*

          Make 1

Step 7 Sew the 1-1/2 x 2-1/2-inch **GOLD DOT** rectangle to the top edge of the 2-1/2 x 4-1/2-inch **GREEN DIAGONAL PRINT** rectangle and sew the 2-1/2 x 5-1/2-inch **GOLD DOT** rectangles to the side edges of the unit; press. <u>At this point the door unit should measure 5-1/2 x 6-1/2-inches.</u> Sew the Step 6 window unit to the left edge of the door unit; press. <u>At this point the unit should measure 5-1/2 x 11-1/2-inches.</u>

 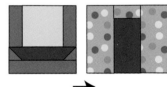

Make 1

          Make 1

Step 8 Sew the units together to make the house block; press. <u>At this point the house block should measure 11-1/2 x 12-1/2-inches.</u> The window panes can be outline stitched at this time.

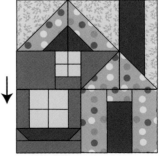

House Block Assembly Diagram

Outline Stitch

Borders

*Note: Yardage given allows for border strips to be cut on crosswise grain. Refer to **Borders** on page 187 for complete instructions.*

Cutting

From **CHESTNUT PRINT**:

• Cut 2, 1-1/2 x 44-inch inner border strips

From **BLUE PRINT**:

• Cut 4, 3-1/2-inch corner squares
• Cut 2, 1-1/2 x 44-inch middle border strips

From **GOLD/BLUE FLORAL**:

• Cut 2, 3-1/2 x 44-inch outer border strips

Attaching Borders

Step 1 Attach 1-1/2-inch wide **CHESTNUT** inner border strips.

Step 2 Attach 1-1/2-inch wide **BLUE** middle border strips.

Step 3 Attach 3-1/2-inch wide **GOLD/BLUE FLORAL** top/bottom outer border strips.

Step 4 For side outer borders, measure the quilt including the seam allowances, but not the top/bottom borders. Cut the remaining 3-1/2-inch **GOLD/BLUE FLORAL** side border strips to this length. Sew the 3-1/2-inch **BLUE** corner squares to each end of the border strips; press. Sew the borders to the quilt; press.

Putting It All Together

Trim batting and backing so they are 6-inches larger than quilt top. Refer to *Finishing the Quilt* on page 189 for complete instructions.

Quilting Suggestions:

• House block - in-the-ditch and echo quilting

• Narrow borders - in-the-ditch

• Outer border - channel stitching

Binding

Cutting

From **GREEN DIAGONAL PRINT**:

• Cut 3, 2-3/4 x 44-inch strips.

Sew binding to quilt using a 3/8-inch seam allowance. This measurement will produce a 1/2-inch wide finished double binding. Refer to *Binding* and *Diagonal Piecing* on page 189 for complete instructions.

Three-Patch

48-inches square

Fabrics & Supplies

1/4 yard **each of 16 ASSORTED PRINTS** for pieced blocks

1-1/4 yards **LARGE FLORAL** for border

1/2 yard **GREEN PRINT** for binding

3 yards for backing

quilt batting, at least 52-inches square

Before beginning this project, read through **Getting Started** *on page 181.*

Three-Patch Blocks

Makes 4 blocks

Cutting

From *each* of the **16 ASSORTED PRINTS**:
* Cut 1, 4-1/2 x 44-inch strip. From strip cut:

  2, 4-1/2 x 8-1/2-inch rectangles

  4, 4-1/2-inch squares

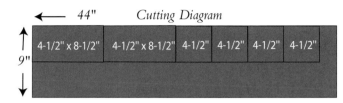

← 44" *Cutting Diagram*

9" | 4-1/2" x 8-1/2" | 4-1/2" x 8-1/2" | 4-1/2" | 4-1/2" | 4-1/2" | 4-1/2" |

Piecing

Refer to arrows on diagrams for pressing.

Step 1 With right sides together, position a 4-1/2-inch **PRINT** square on a 4-1/2 x 8-1/2-inch **PRINT** rectangle. Draw a diagonal line on the square; stitch on the line, trim, and press. Repeat this process at the opposite corner of the rectangle with another 4-1/2-inch **PRINT** square. At this point each unit should measure 4-1/2 x 8-1/2-inches.

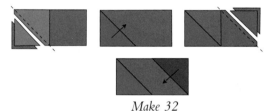

Make 32

Step 2 Sew 8 of the Step 1 units together to make a block; press. At this point each block should measure 16-1/2-inches square.

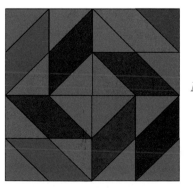

Make 4

Step 3 Referring to quilt illustration on page 81, sew the blocks together; press. At this point the quilt center should measure 32-1/2-inches square.

Border

Note: *Yardage given allows for border strips to be cut on crosswise grain. Diagonally piece strips as needed referring to* **Diagonal Piecing** *instructions page 189. Read through* **Border** *instructions on page 187 for general instructions on adding borders.*

Cutting

From **LARGE FLORAL**:

• Cut 5, 8-1/2 x 44-inch border strips
  Attach 8-1/2-inch wide **LARGE FLORAL** border strips.

Putting It All Together

Cut the 3 yard length of backing fabric in half crosswise to make 2, 1-1/2 yard lengths. Refer to **Finishing the Quilt** on page 189 for complete instructions. Our quilt was quilted with an allover design.

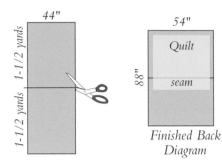

Binding

Cutting

From **GREEN PRINT**:

• Cut 5, 2-3/4 x 44-inch strips.

Sew binding to quilt using a 3/8-inch seam allowance. This measurement will produce a 1/2-inch wide finished double binding. Refer to **Binding** and **Diagonal Piecing** on page 189 for complete instructions.

Three Patch Wall Quilt

48-inches square

Pumpkin, Pumpkin

40 x 46-inches

Fabrics & Supplies

(9) 6-1/2 x 7-inch rectangles
COORDINATING ORANGE PRINTS for pumpkin blocks

1-1/4 yards   **GREEN PRINT** for stems, outer border

1/4 yard   **BEIGE PRINT** for background

5/8 yard   **BLACK PRINT** for lattice strips, inner border

1/2 yard   **BLACK PRINT** for binding

1-1/2 yards for backing

quilt batting, at least 46 x 52-inches

Before beginning this project, read through **Getting Started** *on page 181.*

Pumpkin Blocks

Makes 9 blocks

Cutting

From *each* of the
9 COORDINATING ORANGE PRINTS:
• Cut 2, 3-1/2 x 6-1/2-inch rectangles

From **GREEN PRINT**:
• Cut 2, 1-1/2 x 44-inch strips. From strips cut:
    45, 1-1/2-inch squares

From **BEIGE PRINT**:
• Cut 5, 1-1/2 x 44-inch strips. From strips cut:
    27, 1-1/2 x 3-1/2-inch rectangles
    9, 1-1/2 x 2-1/2-inch rectangles
    36, 1-1/2-inch squares

Piecing

Refer to arrows on diagrams for pressing.

Step 1   With right sides together, position a 1-1/2-inch **GREEN** square on the corner of a 1-1/2 x 3-1/2-inch **BEIGE** rectangle. Draw a diagonal line on the square; stitch on line. Trim seam allowance to 1/4-inch; press. Make 18 units. Sew the units together in pairs; press.

Make 18   *Make 9*

Step 2   Sew together a 1-1/2 x 3-1/2-inch **BEIGE** rectangle, a 1-1/2-inch **GREEN** square, and a 1-1/2 x 2-1/2-inch **BEIGE** rectangle; press. Make 9 units. Sew the units to the bottom edge of the Step 1 units; press.

Make 9   
Make 9

Step 3   With right sides together, position a 1-1/2-inch **GREEN** square on the upper right corner of a 3-1/2 x 6-1/2-inch **ORANGE** rectangle. Draw a diagonal line on the square; stitch on line, trim, and press. Repeat this process at the upper left and lower left corners of the rectangle using 1-1/2-inch **BEIGE** squares.

Make 9

Step 4 With right sides together, position a 1-1/2-inch **GREEN** square on the upper left corner of a 3-1/2 x 6-1/2-inch **ORANGE** rectangle. Draw a diagonal line on the square; stitch on line, trim, and press. Repeat this process at the upper right and lower right corners of the rectangle using 1-1/2-inch **BEIGE** squares.

Make 9

Step 5 Sew together the Step 3 and Step 4 units in pairs; press. Sew the Step 2 units to the top edge of this unit; press. <u>At this point each pumpkin block should measure 6-1/2 x 8-1/2-inches.</u>

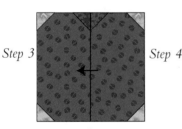

Step 3   *Step 4*

Make 9

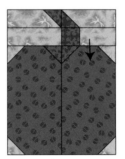

Make 9 pumpkin blocks

Quilt Center and Borders

*Note: Yardage given allows for border strips to be cut on the crosswise grain. Diagonally piece the strips as needed, referring to **Diagonal Piecing** on page 189. Read through **Border** instructions on page 187 for instructions on adding borders.*

Cutting

From **BLACK PRINT**:
- Cut 2, 2-1/2 x 44-inch strips. From strips cut:
  6, 2-1/2 x 8-1/2-inch lattice segments
- Cut 6, 2-1/2 x 44-inch lattice/inner border strips

From **GREEN PRINT**:
- Cut 5, 7-1/2 x 44-inch outer border strips

Quilt Center Assembly

Step 1 Sew together 3 pumpkin blocks and 2 of the 2-1/2 x 8-1/2-inch **BLACK** lattice segments; press. <u>At this point each block row should measure 8-1/2 x 22-1/2-inches.</u>

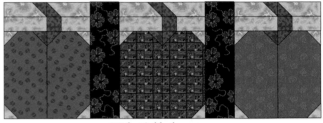

Make 3 block rows

Step 2 Cut 4 of the 2-1/2-inch wide **BLACK** lattice/inner border strips to 22-1/2-inches long. Sew together the 3 block rows and the 4 lattice/inner border strips. Press seam allowances toward lattice/inner border strips.

Step 3 Attach 2-1/2-inch wide **BLACK** side inner border strips.

Step 4 Attach 7-1/2-inch wide **GREEN** outer border strips.

Putting It All Together

Trim batting and backing so they are 6-inches larger than quilt top. Refer to **Finishing the Quilt** on page 189 for complete instructions.

Quilting Suggestions:

- Pumpkins – **TB52 – 5-1/2" Oak Leaf**

- Stems – in-the-ditch

- **BEIGE** – stipple

- **BLACK** inner border – **TB64 – 1-1/2" Nordic Scroll**

- **GREEN** outer border – **TB26 – 7" Acorn Vine**

THIMBLEBERRIES® *quilt stencils by Quilting Creations International are available at your local quilt shop or visit www.quiltingcreations.com.*

Binding

Cutting

From **BLACK PRINT**:

• Cut 5, 2-3/4 x 44-inch strips.

Sew binding to quilt using a 3/8-inch seam allowance. This measurement will produce a 1/2-inch wide finished double binding. Refer to **Binding** and **Diagonal Piecing** on page 189 for complete instructions.

Pumpkin, Pumpkin Wall Quilt

40 x 46-inches

Little Acorn

17-inches square

Fabrics & Supplies

5 x 8-inch piece	**MEDIUM BROWN PRINT** for acorn base
5 x 8-inch piece	**BROWN/GOLD PRINT** for acorn cap
1/8 yard	**BEIGE PRINT** for background
1/8 yard	**RUST PRINT** for pieced border
1/8 yard	**DARK BROWN PRINT** for pieced border, corner squares, stem appliqué
1/4 yard	**LARGE GREEN FLORAL** for outer border
1/8 yard	**GOLD PRINT** for leaf appliqués
1/4 yard	**ORANGE PRINT** for binding

2/3 yard for backing

quilt batting, at least 23-inches square

paper-backed fusible web

pearl cotton or machine embroidery thread
      for decorative stitches: black, gold

template material

tear-away fabric stabilizer

*Before beginning this project,
read through **Getting Started** on page 181.*

*read through **Getting Started** on page 181.*

Quilt Center

Cutting

From MEDIUM BROWN PRINT:
• Cut 1, 4 x 5-1/2-inch rectangle

From BROWN/GOLD PRINT:
• Cut 1, 3 x 6-1/2-inch rectangle

From BEIGE PRINT:
• Cut 1, 2-1/2 x 44-inch strip. From strip cut:
      2, 2-1/2-inch squares
      2, 1 x 4-inch rectangles
      2, 1-inch squares

• Cut 1, 1-1/2 x 44-inch strip. From strip cut:
      2, 1-1/2 x 8-1/2-inch rectangles
      2, 1-1/2 x 6-1/2-inch rectangles
      2, 1-1/2-inch squares

Piecing

Refer to arrows on diagrams for pressing.

Step 1 With right sides together, position 2-1/2-inch
BEIGE squares on both bottom corners of the
4 x 5-1/2-inch **MEDIUM BROWN** rectangle.
Draw a diagonal line on the squares and stitch on
the lines. Trim seam allowances to 1/4-inch; press.
Sew 1 x 4-inch **BEIGE** rectangles to both side
edges; press. <u>At this point the acorn base should
measure 4 x 6-1/2-inches.</u>

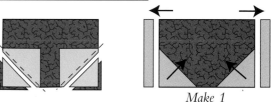

Make 1

Step 2 With right sides together, position 1-1/2-inch
BEIGE squares on both upper corners of the
3 x 6-1/2-inch **BROWN/GOLD** rectangle. Draw
a diagonal line on the squares; stitch, trim, and press.
Position 1-inch **BEIGE** squares on both bottom
corners of the rectangle. Draw a diagonal line on
the squares; stitch, trim, and press. <u>At this point the
acorn cap should measure 3 x 6-1/2-inches.</u>

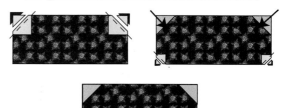

Make 1

Step 3 Sew the Step 2 acorn cap to the top edge of the
Step 1 acorn base; press. <u>At this point the acorn unit
should measure 6-1/2-inches square.</u>

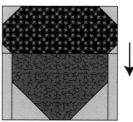

Make 1

Step 4 Referring to the quilt illustration on page 89, sew the 1-1/2 x 6-1/2-inch **BEIGE** rectangles to the top/bottom edges of the acorn unit; press. Sew the 1-1/2 x 8-1/2-inch **BEIGE** rectangles to both side edges of the unit; press. At this point the quilt center should measure 8-1/2-inches square.

Borders

Note: *Yardage given allows for border strips to be cut on the crosswise grain. Diagonally piece the strips as needed, referring to Diagonal Piecing on page 189. Read through Border instructions on page 187 for instructions on adding borders.*

Cutting

From **RUST PRINT**:

• Cut 2, 1 x 44-inch strips

From **DARK BROWN PRINT**:

• Cut 1, 2 x 12-inch strip. From strip cut:
    4, 2-inch corner squares
• Cut 1, 1 x 44-inch strip

From **LARGE GREEN FLORAL**:

• Cut 2, 3-1/2 x 44-inch outer border strips

Assembling and Attaching Borders

Press seam allowances toward borders just added.

Step 1 Aligning long edges, sew 1 x 44-inch **RUST** strips to both side edges of the 1 x 44-inch **DARK BROWN** strip. Cut strip set into segments.

Crosscut 4, 8-1/2-inch long segments

Step 2 Sew 2 of the Step 1 segments to the top/bottom edges of the quilt center; press. Sew 2-inch **DARK BROWN** corner squares to both ends of the remaining Step 1 segments; press. Sew the strips to the side edges of the quilt center; press. At this point the quilt center should measure 11-1/2-inches square.

Step 3 Attach 3-1/2-inch wide **LARGE GREEN FLORAL** outer border strips.

Paper-Backed Fusible Web Appliqué

Step 1 Make templates using shapes on page 89. Trace shapes on paper side of fusible web.

Step 2 When you are fusing a large shape like the leaf, fuse just the outer edges of the shape so the center is softer to the touch and it will not look stiff when finished. Cut away fusible web about 3/8-inch inside the shape.

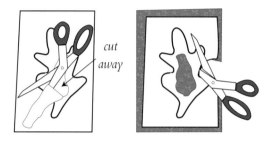

Step 3 Following manufacturer's instructions, fuse shapes to wrong side of fabrics chosen for appliqués. Let fabric cool and cut along traced line. Peel away paper backing from fusible web. Position appliqué shapes on quilt center.

Step 4 For machine appliqué, we suggest pinning a square of tear-away stabilizer to backside of quilt center so it will lay flat when machine applique is complete. We machine blanket stitched around shapes using embroidery thread. If you like, you could hand blanket stitch around shapes with pearl cotton.

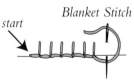

Blanket Stitch

start

Note: *To prevent hand blanket stitches from "rolling off" edges of appliqué shapes, take an extra backstitch in same place as you made blanket stitch, going around outer curves, corners, and points. For straight edges, taking a backstitch every inch is enough.*

Putting It All Together

Trim backing and batting so they are 6-inches larger than the quilt top. Refer to the **Finishing the Quilt** on page 189 for complete instructions.

Quilting Suggestions:

- Appliqué shapes – in-the-ditch
- Acorn – in-the-ditch and echo quilting
- Pieced border – in-the-ditch
- Outer border – **TB28 – 3" Leaf Sketch**

THIMBLEBERRIES® *quilt stencils by Quilting Creations International are available at your local quilt shop or visit www.quiltingcreations.com.*

Binding

Cutting

From **ORANGE PRINT**:

- Cut 2, 2-3/4 x 44-inch strips

Sew binding to quilt using a 3/8-inch seam allowance. This measurement will produce a 1/2-inch wide finished double binding. Refer to **Binding** and **Diagonal Piecing** on page 189 for complete instructions.

Appliqué Pieces

The appliqué shapes are reversed for tracing purposes. When the appliqué is finished it will appear as in the illustration.

Leaf

Trace 2 onto fusible web

Stem

Trace 1 onto fusible web

Little Acorn
Wall Quilt

17-inches square

Boo!

14-inches square

Fabrics & Supplies

10-1/2-inch square	**BEIGE PRINT** for appliqué foundation
1/8 yard	**PLUM PRINT** for border
7-inch square	**ORANGE PRINT** for pumpkin appliqué
1/8 yard	**BLACK PRINT** for pumpkin appliqué, lettering
3/8 yard	**BLACK PRINT** for binding

5/8 yard for backing

quilt batting, at least 20-inches square

paper-backed fusible web

pearl cotton or machine embroidery thread for decorative stitches: black

template material

tear-away fabric stabilizer

*Before beginning this project, read through **Getting Started** on page 181.*

Paper-Backed Fusible Web Appliqué

Step 1 Make templates using shapes on pages 92 and 93. Trace shapes on paper side of fusible web.

Step 2 When you are fusing a large shape like the pumpkin, fuse just the outer edges of the shape so the center is softer to the touch and it will not look stiff when finished. Cut away fusible web about 3/8-inch inside the shape.

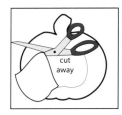

Step 3 Following manufacturer's instructions, fuse shapes to wrong side of fabrics chosen for appliqués. Let fabric cool and cut along traced line. Peel away paper backing from fusible web. Position appliqué shapes on 10-1/2-inch **BEIGE** appliqué foundation square.

Step 4 For machine appliqué, we suggest pinning a square of tear-away stabilizer to backside of the square so it will lay flat when machine appliqué is complete. Use a decorative stitch and embroidery thread to secure the shapes in place. Our sample was hand blanket stitched using pearl cotton.

Blanket Stitch

Note: To prevent hand blanket stitches from "rolling off" edges of appliqué shapes, take an extra backstitch in same place as you made blanket stitch, going around outer curves, corners, and points. For straight edges, taking a backstitch every inch is enough.

Border

*Note: Yardage given allows for border strips to be cut on the crosswise grain. Read through **Borders** on page 187 for instructions on adding borders.*

Cutting

From **PLUM PRINT**:

• Cut 2, 2-1/2 x 44-inch border strips.

Attach 2-1/2-inch wide **PLUM** border strips.

Putting It All Together

Trim backing and batting so they are 6-inches larger than the quilt top. Refer to *Finishing the Quilt* on page 189 for complete instructions.

Quilting Suggestions:

- Appliqué shapes - in-the-ditch
- **BEIGE** background - crosshatch
- **PLUM** border - channel stitching

Binding

Cutting

From **BLACK PRINT**:

- Cut 2, 2-3/4 x 44-inch strips

Sew binding to quilt using a 3/8-inch seam allowance. This measurement will produce a 1/2-inch wide finished double binding. Refer to *Binding* and *Diagonal Piecing* on page 189 for complete instructions.

Appliqué Pieces

The appliqué shapes are reversed for tracing purposes.
When the appliqué is finished it will appear as in the illustration.

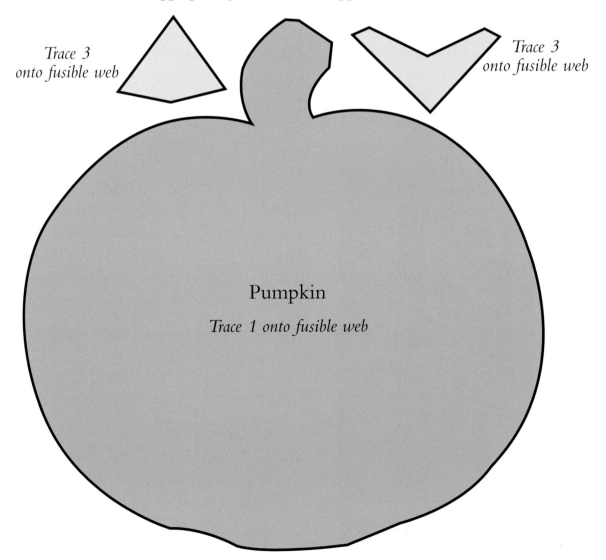

Trace 3 onto fusible web

Trace 3 onto fusible web

Pumpkin

Trace 1 onto fusible web

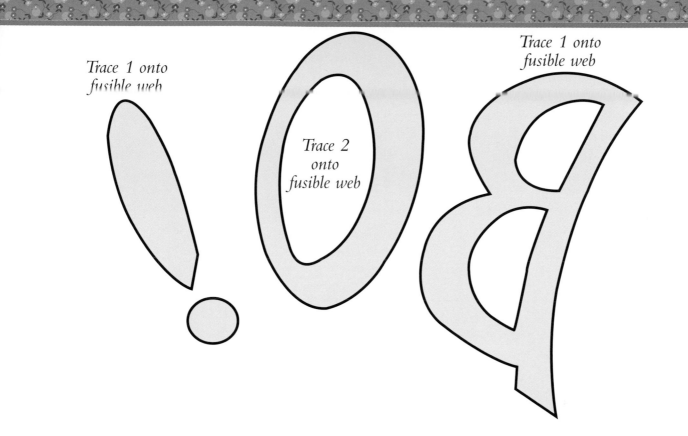

Trace 1 onto fusible web

Trace 2 onto fusible web

Trace 1 onto fusible web

Teeny, Tiny Baskets

12-inches square

Fabrics & Supplies

3 x 9-inch piece   *each* of **4 COORDINATING PRINTS** for basket blocks

1/8 yard   **BEIGE PRINT** for background and inner border

1/4 yard   **GREEN PRINT** for middle border, binding

1/8 yard   **LARGE ROSE FLORAL** for outer border

18-inch square for backing

quilt batting, at least 18-inches square

*Before beginning this project, read through **Getting Started** on page 181.*

Basket Blocks

Makes 4 blocks

From *each* of the **4 COORDINATING PRINTS**:
- Cut 1, 2-7/8-inch square.

  Cut squares in half diagonally to make 2 triangles of each color. You will be using only 1 triangle of each color.

2-7/8"

- Cut 1, 1 x 4-inch *bias* strip for each basket handle

From **BEIGE PRINT**:
- Cut 2, 2-7/8-inch squares. Cut squares in half diagonally to make 4 triangles.

2-7/8"

Piecing

Step 1   To make a basket handle, fold a 1 x 4-inch *bias* strip in half lengthwise with wrong sides together; press. To keep raw edges aligned, stitch a scant 1/4-inch away from edges. Fold strip in half again so raw edges are hidden by the first folded edge; press. Hand baste if needed.

Step 2   Referring to handle placement diagram on page 96, position prepared basket handle on a **BEIGE** triangle staying 3/8-inch away from triangle edge; hand baste or pin. Hand appliqué basket handle in place. Repeat to make 4 handle units. Sew the corresponding **PRINT** triangles to the bottom edge of each handle unit; press. Repeat to make 4 basket units. <u>At this point each block should measure 2-1/2-inches square.</u>

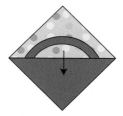

Make 4 basket blocks

*Handle Placement
Diagram*

Step 3 Sew 4 basket blocks together; press. <u>At this point the quilt center should measure 4-1/2-inches square.</u>

Borders

Note: Yardage given allows for border strips to be cut on crosswise grain. Read through **Border** *instructions on page 187 for general instructions on adding borders.*

Cutting

From **BEIGE PRINT**:
• Cut 1, 1-1/2 x 36-inch inner border strip

From **GREEN PRINT**:
• Cut 1, 1 x 44-inch middle border strip

From **LARGE ROSE FLORAL**:
• Cut 1, 3 x 44-inch outer border strip

Attaching Borders

Step 1 Attach 1-1/2-inch wide **BEIGE** inner border strips.

Step 2 Attach 1-inch wide **GREEN PRINT** middle border strips.

Step 3 Attach 3-inch wide **LARGE ROSE FLORAL** outer border strips.

Putting It All Together

Trim backing and batting so they are 6-inches larger than quilt top. Refer to *Finishing the Quilt* on page 189 for complete instructions.

Quilting Suggestions:

• Baskets – in-the-ditch

• Narrow borders – in-the-ditch

• Outer border – **TB74 – 2-1/2" Beadwork**

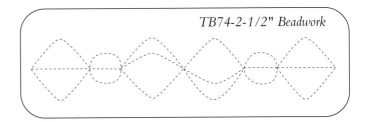

TB74-2-1/2" Beadwork

THIMBLEBERRIES® *quilt stencils by Quilting Creations International are available at your local quilt shop or visit www.quiltingcreations.com.*

Binding

Cutting

From **GREEN PRINT**:
• Cut 2, 2-3/4 x 44-inch strips

Sew binding to quilt using a 3/8-inch seam allowance. This measurement will produce a 1/2-inch wide finished double binding. Refer to *Binding* and *Diagonal Piecing* on page 189 for complete instructions.

Teeny, Tiny Baskets Wall Quilt

12-inches square

Flannel Quick Quilt

56 x 64-inches

Fabrics & Supplies

1-1/3 yards   **ORANGE/GREEN DOT** for center panel, second middle border

1/3 yard   **GREEN/BROWN GEOMETRIC PRINT** for inner border

3/8 yard   **ORANGE/BROWN STRIPE** for first middle border

1/2 yard   **GREEN PRINT** for checkerboard border

1/2 yard   **ORANGE/WHITE GEOMETRIC PRINT** for checkerboard border

1-1/2 yards   **YELLOW/ORANGE GEOMETRIC PRINT** for outer border

1-1/3 yards   **ORANGE/BROWN STRIPE** for wide binding

3-1/2 yards for backing

quilt batting, at least 62 x 70-inches

*Before beginning this project,
read through **Getting Started** on page 181.*

Center Panel and Borders

Note: *Yardage given allows for border strips to be cut on crosswise grain. Diagonally piece the strips as needed, referring to* **Diagonal Piecing** *instructions on page 189. Read through* **Border** *instructions on page 187 for general instructions on adding borders.*

Cutting

From **ORANGE/GREEN DOT**:
• Cut 1, 20-1/2 x 28-1/2-inch center rectangle
• Cut 5, 4-1/2 x 44-inch second middle
    border strips

From **GREEN/BROWN GEOMETRIC PRINT**:
• Cut 3, 2-1/2 x 44-inch inner border strips

From **ORANGE/BROWN STRIPE**:
• Cut 4, 2-1/2 x 44-inch first middle border strips

From **GREEN PRINT**:
• Cut 3, 4-1/2 x 44-inch strips for checkerboard border

From **ORANGE/WHITE GEOMETRIC PRINT**:
• Cut 3, 4-1/2 x 44-inch strips for checkerboard border

From **YELLOW/ORANGE GEOMETRIC PRINT**:
• Cut 7, 6-1/2 x 44-inch outer border strips

Assembling and Attaching the Borders

Press border strips toward borders just added.

Step 1   Attach 2-1/2-inch wide **GREEN/BROWN GEOMETRIC PRINT** inner border strips to 20-1/2 x 28-1/2-inch **ORANGE/GREEN DOT** center panel.

Step 2   Attach 2-1/2-inch wide **ORANGE/BROWN STRIPE** first middle border strips.

Step 3   Aligning long edges, sew together the 4-1/2 x 44-inch **GREEN** and **ORANGE/WHITE GEOMETRIC PRINT** strips in pairs. Make 3 strip sets. Press strip sets referring to **Hints and Helps for Pressing Strip Sets** on page 187. Cut strip sets into segments.

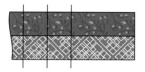

Crosscut 20, 4-1/2-inch wide segments

Step 4 For the top/bottom checkerboard borders, sew together 4 of the segments. Remove 1 of the 4-1/2-inch green squares from the end of the strip; press. Make 2 border strips. Sew the checkerboard borders to the top/bottom edges of the quilt center; press.

Make 2 for top/bottom borders

Step 5 For the side checkerboard borders, sew together 6 of the segments. Remove 1 of the 4-1/2-inch **ORANGE/WHITE GEOMETRIC PRINT** squares from the end of the strip; press. Make 2 border strips. Sew the checkerboard borders to the side edges of the quilt center; press.

Make 2 for side borders

Step 6 Attach 4-1/2-inch wide **ORANGE/GREEN DOT** second middle border strips.

Step 7 Attach 6-1/2-inch wide **YELLOW/ORANGE GEOMETRIC PRINT** outer border strips.

Putting It All Together

Cut 3-1/2 yard length of backing fabric in half crosswise to make 2, 1-3/4 yard lengths. Refer to *Finishing the Quilt* on page 189 for complete instructions. Our quilt was quilted with an allover quilt design.

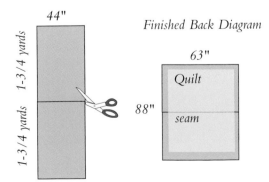

Binding
Cutting

From **ORANGE/BROWN STRIPE**:
• Cut 7, 6-1/2 x 44-inch strips

Sew binding to quilt using a scant 1-inch seam allowance. This measurement will produce a 1-inch wide finished double binding. Refer to *Binding* and *Diagonal Piecing* on page 189 for complete instructions.

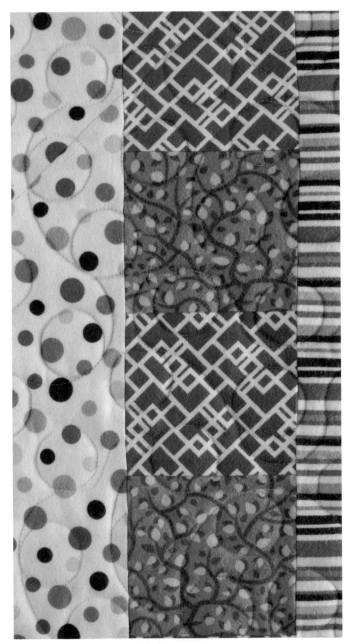

Quilting Suggestion

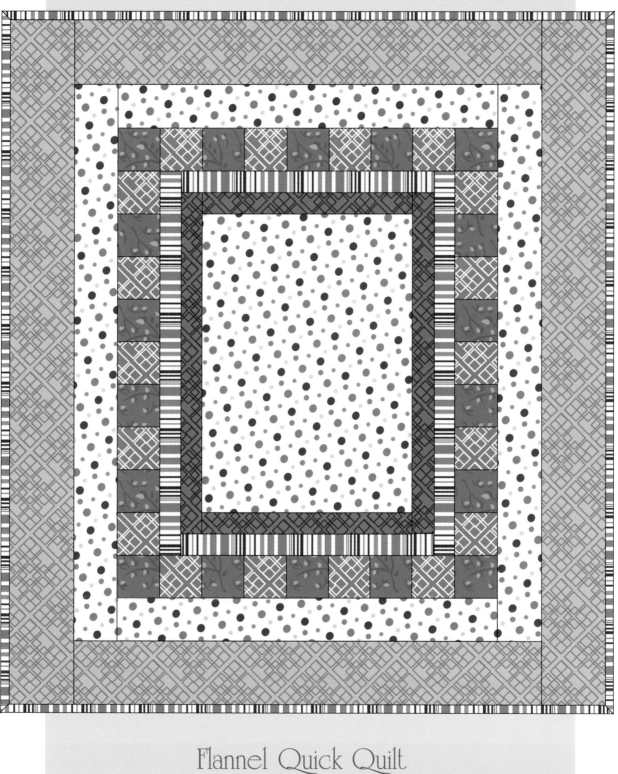

Flannel Quick Quilt
56 x 64-inches

Star Studded

54 x 58-inches

Fabrics & Supplies

5/8 yard   **DARK RED PRINT** for star blocks

1 yard   **GOLD PRINT** for star blocks, hourglass blocks, middle border

3/4 yard   **BEIGE PRINT** for background

1-1/2 yards   **BLUE PRINT** for hourglass blocks, outer border

3/4 yard   **RED DIAGONAL PRINT** for lattice, inner border

1/2 yard   **RED DIAGONAL PRINT** for binding

3-1/3 yards for backing

quilt batting, at least 60 x 64-inches

*Before beginning this project,
read through **Getting Started** on page 181.*

Star Blocks

Makes 3 blocks

Cutting

From **DARK RED PRINT**:
- Cut 1, 4-1/2 x 44-inch strip. From strip cut:
  9, 4-1/2-inch squares. Set aside 6 of the squares for the side star blocks.
- Cut 2, 2-1/2 x 44-inch strips. From strips cut:
  24, 2-1/2-inch squares

From **GOLD PRINT**:
- Cut 1, 2-7/8 x 44-inch strip
- Cut 5, 2-1/2 x 44-inch strips. From strips cut:
  24, 2-1/2 x 4-1/2-inch rectangles
  24, 2-1/2-inch squares

From **BEIGE PRINT**:
- Cut 1, 2-7/8 x 44-inch strip
- Cut 3, 2-1/2 x 44-inch strips. From strips cut:
  12, 2-1/2 x 4-1/2-inch rectangles
  24, 2-1/2-inch squares

Piecing

Refer to arrows on diagrams for pressing.

Step 1   With right sides together, position a 2-1/2-inch **DARK RED** square on the corner of a 2-1/2 x 4-1/2-inch **GOLD** rectangle. Draw a diagonal line on the square; stitch on the line. Trim seam allowance to 1/4-inch; press. Repeat this process at the opposite corner of the rectangle; press.

Make 12

Step 2   With right sides together, position a 2-1/2-inch **GOLD** square on the corner of a 2-1/2 x 4-1/2-inch **BEIGE** rectangle. Draw a diagonal line on the square; stitch on the line, trim, and press. Repeat this process at the opposite corner of the rectangle; press.

Make 12

Step 3 Sew Step 1 and Step 2 star points together in pairs; press. Make 12 star point units. Sew star point units to the top/bottom edges of 3 of the 4-1/2-inch **DARK RED** squares; press. At this point each unit should measure 4-1/2 x 12-1/2-inches.

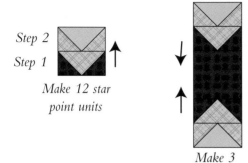

Step 2
Step 1

Make 12 star point units

Make 3

Step 4 With right sides together, position a 2-1/2-inch **BEIGE** square on the right corner of a 2-1/2 x 4-1/2-inch **GOLD** rectangle. Draw a diagonal line on the square; stitch on the line, trim, and press.

Make 12

Step 5 With right sides together, layer the 2-7/8 x 44-inch **BEIGE** and **GOLD** strips together. Press together, but do not sew. Cut the layered strip into squares. Cut the layered squares in half diagonally to make 12 sets of triangles. Stitch 1/4-inch from the diagonal edge of each triangle set; press.

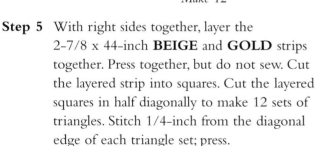

Crosscut 6, 2-7/8-inch squares

Make 12, 2-1/2-inch triangle-pieced squares

Step 6 Sew a 2-1/2-inch **BEIGE** square to the top edge of each triangle-pieced square; press. Sew Step 4 units to the left edge of the units; press. At this point each unit should measure 4-1/2-inches square.

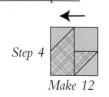

Step 4

Make 12

Step 7 Sew Step 6 units to the top/bottom edges of the remaining star point units; press. Make 6 units. Sew the units to the side edges of the Step 3 units; press. At this point each center star block should measure 12-1/2-inches square.

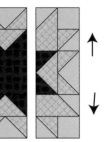 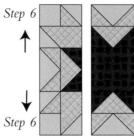 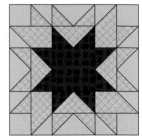

Step 6

Step 6

Step 3

Make 3 center star blocks

Side Star Blocks

Makes 6 blocks

Cutting

From **DARK RED PRINT**:

• Cut 3, 2-1/2 x 44-inch strips. From strips cut:
    48, 2-1/2-inch squares

The 6, 4-1/2-inch squares were cut previously.

From **BEIGE PRINT**:

• Cut 5, 2-1/2 x 44-inch strips. From strips cut:
    24, 2-1/2 x 4-1/2-inch rectangles
    24, 2-1/2-inch squares

Piecing

Refer to arrows on diagrams for pressing.

Step 1 With right sides together, position a 2-1/2-inch **DARK RED** square on the corner of a 2-1/2 x 4-1/2-inch **BEIGE** rectangle. Draw a diagonal line on the square; stitch on the line. Trim seam allowance to 1/4-inch; press. Repeat this process at the opposite corner of the rectangle; press.

Make 24

Step 2 Sew star point units to the top/bottom edges of 6 of the 4-1/2-inch **DARK RED** squares; press. Sew 2-1/2-inch **BEIGE** squares to both sides of the remaining star point units; press.

Sew the star point units to the square unit; press. At this point each side star block should measure 8-1/2-inches square.

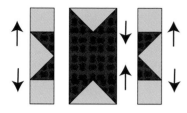 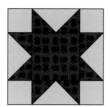

Make 6 side star blocks

Hourglass Blocks

Makes 4 blocks

Cutting

From **BLUE PRINT**:

• Cut 1, 9-1/4 x 44-inch strip. From strip cut:
    2, 9-1/4-inch squares

From **GOLD PRINT**:

• Cut 1, 9-1/4 x 44-inch strip. From strip cut:
    2, 9-1/4-inch squares

Piecing

Refer to arrows on diagrams for pressing.

Step 1 With right sides together, layer the 9-1/4-inch **BLUE** and **GOLD** squares in pairs. Press together, but do not sew. Cut layered squares diagonally into quarters to make 8 sets of triangles.

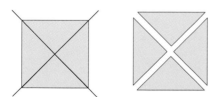

Step 2 Stitch along the same **bias** edge of each triangle set being careful not to stretch the triangles; press. Sew the triangle sets together in pairs to make hourglass blocks; press. At this point each hourglass block should measure 8-1/2-inches square.

Bias edges

Make 8 triangle units   *Make 4 hourglass units*

Quilt Center

Cutting

From **RED DIAGONAL PRINT**:

• Cut 2, 4-1/2 x 44-inch vertical lattice strips
• Cut 1, 2-1/2 x 44-inch strip. From strip cut:
    2, 2-1/2 x 12-1/2-inch horizontal lattice strips

Quilt Center Assembly

Step 1 Referring to quilt center assembly diagram, sew together the 3 center star blocks and the 2, 2-1/2 x 12-1/2-inch **RED DIAGONAL PRINT** horizontal lattice strips; press. At this point the center block row should measure 12-1/2 x 40-1/2-inches.

Step 2 Cut the 4-1/2 x 44-inch **RED DIAGONAL PRINT** vertical lattice strips to 40-1/2-inches long. Sew the vertical lattice strips to the side edges of the center block row; press.

Step 3 Sew together 3 side star blocks and 2 hourglass blocks; press. Make 2 block rows. At this point each side block row should measure 8-1/2 x 40-1/2-inches long.

Step 4 Referring to quilt center assembly, sew the block rows together; press. At this point the quilt center should measure 36-1/2 x 40-1/2-inches.

Quilt Center Assembly Diagram

Borders

Note: Yardage given allows for border strips to be cut on crosswise grain. Diagonally piece the strips as needed, referring to Diagonal Piecing instructions on page 189. Read through Border instructions on page 187 for general instructions on adding borders.

Cutting

From **RED DIAGONAL PRINT**:

• Cut 5, 2-1/2 x 44-inch inner border strips

From **GOLD PRINT**:

• Cut 5, 1-1/2 x 44-inch middle border strips

From **BLUE PRINT**:

• Cut 5 to 6, 6-1/2 x 44-inch outer border strips

Attaching Borders

Press border strips toward borders just added.

Step 1 Attach 2-1/2-inch wide **RED DIAGONAL PRINT** inner border strips.

Step 2 Attach 1-1/2-inch wide **GOLD** middle border strips.

Step 3 Attach 6-1/2-inch wide **BLUE** outer border strips.

Putting It All Together

Cut 3-1/3 yard length of backing fabric in half crosswise to make 2, 1-2/3 yard lengths. Refer to *Finishing the Quilt* on page 189 for complete instructions.

Finished Back Diagram

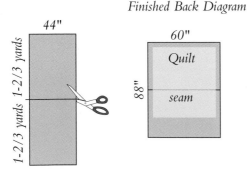

44"

1-2/3 yards 1-2/3 yards

1-2/3 yards

60"

88"

Quilt

seam

Quilting Suggestions:

• **BEIGE** - stipple

• Center star blocks - point to point

• Side star blocks - point to point

• Hourglass blocks - in-the-ditch and echo quilting

• **RED DIAGONAL PRINT** horizontal lattice - channel stitching

• **RED DIAGONAL PRINT** vertical lattice - **TB76 - 3-1/2" Holly Chain**

• **DARK RED/GOLD** inner/middle borders (quilt as one border) - **TB34 - 2-1/2" Holly Chain**

• **BLUE** outer border - **TB44-5-1/2" Star Vine Border**

• *Point to Point*
• *Echo quilting*
• *In-the-ditch*

• *Echo quilting*
• *In-the-ditch*

THIMBLEBERRIES® *quilt stencils by Quilting Creations International are available at your local quilt shop or visit www.quiltingcreations.com.*

Binding

Cutting

From **RED DIAGONAL PRINT**:

• Cut 6, 2-3/4 x 44-inch strips

Sew binding to quilt using a 3/8-inch seam allowance. This measurement will produce a 1/2-inch wide finished double binding. Refer to *Binding* and *Diagonal Piecing* on page 189 for complete instructions.

Star Studded Quilt

54 x 58-inches

Baby Girl

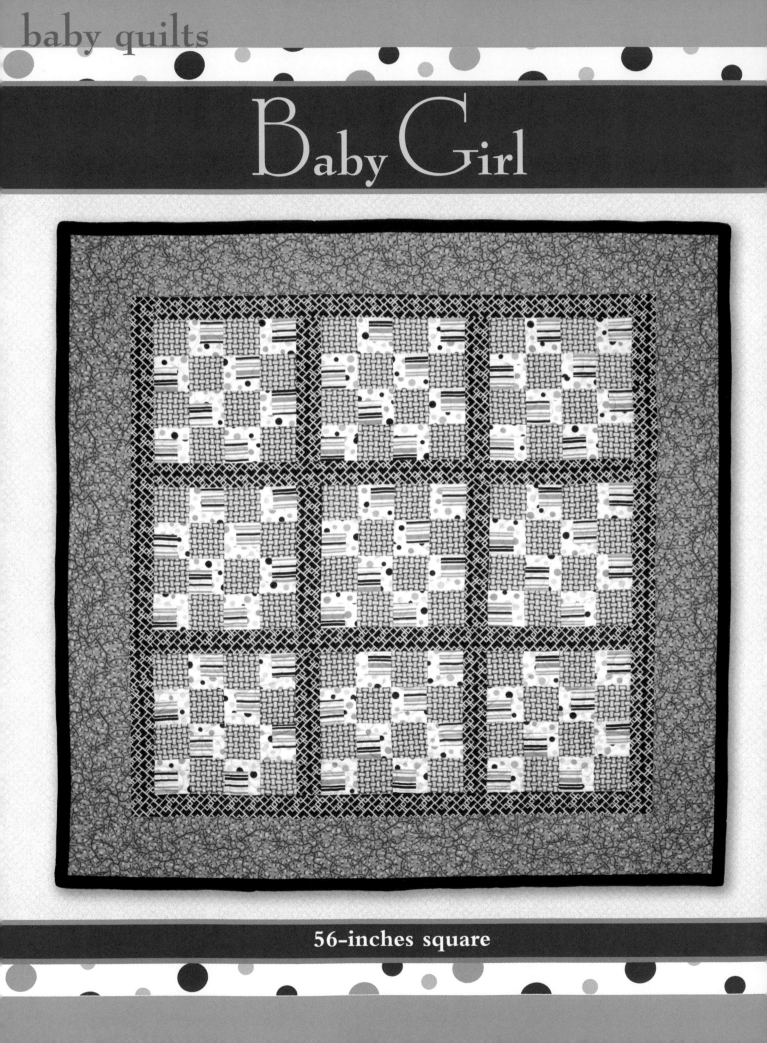

56-inches square

Fabrics & Supplies

1/2 yard	**PINK/BROWN STRIPE** for blocks
5/8 yard	**PINK/BROWN DOT** for blocks
7/8 yard	**PINK/BROWN WEAVE PRINT** for blocks
3/4 yard	**BROWN/PINK GEOMETRIC PRINT** for lattice, inner border
1-1/4 yards	**PINK PRINT** for outer border
1-1/3 yards	**BROWN SOLID** for wide binding

3-1/2 yards for backing

quilt batting, at least 62-inches square

*Before beginning this project,
read through **Getting Started** on page 181.*

Pieced Blocks

Makes 9 blocks

Cutting

From **PINK/BROWN STRIPE**:
• Cut 5, 2-1/2 x 44-inch strips

From **PINK/BROWN DOT**:
• Cut 3, 3-1/2 x 44-inch strips. From strips cut:
    72, 1-1/2 x 3-1/2-inch rectangles
• Cut 5, 1-1/2 x 44-inch strips

From **PINK/BROWN WEAVE PRINT**:
• Cut 7, 3-1/2 x 44-inch strips. From strips cut:
    72, 3-1/2-inch squares

Piecing

Refer to arrows on diagrams for pressing.

Step 1 Aligning long edges, sew together the 1-1/2 x 44-inch **PINK/BROWN DOT** strips and the 2-1/2 x 44-inch **PINK/BROWN STRIPE** strips in pairs; press. Make 5 strip sets. Cut the strip sets into segments. Sew a 1-1/2 x 3-1/2-inch **PINK/BROWN DOT** rectangle to the right edge of each unit; press. At this point each unit should measure 3-1/2-inches square.

Crosscut 72, 2-1/2-inch wide segments

Make 72

Step 2 Referring to the block diagram, sew together 8 Step 1 units and 8, 3-1/2-inch **PINK/BROWN WEAVE PRINT** squares in 4 rows; press. Sew the rows together; press. At this point each block should measure 12-1/2-inches square.

Note: *Pay close attention to the Step 1 block placement.*

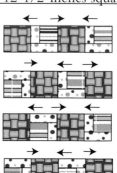

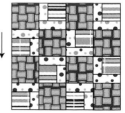

Make 9 blocks

109

Quilt Center

Cutting

From **BROWN/PINK GEOMETRIC PRINT**:

• Cut 4, 2-1/2 x 44-inch strips. From strips cut:
    2, 2-1/2 x 40-1/2-inch lattice strips
    6, 2-1/2 x 12-1/2-inch lattice segments

Quilt Center Assembly

Step 1 Referring to quilt illustration on page 111, sew together 3 of the pieced blocks and 2 of the 2-1/2 x 12-1/2-inch **BROWN/PINK GEOMETRIC PRINT** lattice segments; press. Make 3 block rows. <u>At this point each block row should measure 12-1/2 x 40-1/2-inches.</u>

Step 2 Sew together the block rows and the 2-1/2 x 40-1/2-inch **BROWN/PINK GEOMETRIC PRINT** lattice strips; press. <u>At this point the quilt center should measure 40-1/2-inches square.</u>

Borders

*Note: Yardage given allows for border strips to be cut on crosswise grain. Diagonally piece the strips as needed, referring to **Diagonal Piecing** instructions on page 189. Read through **Border** instructions on page 187 for general instructions on adding borders.*

Cutting

From **BROWN/PINK GEOMETRIC PRINT**:

• Cut 5, 2-1/2 x 44-inch inner border strips

From **PINK PRINT**:

• Cut 6, 6-1/2 x 44-inch outer border strips

Attaching Borders

Step 1 Attach 2-1/2-inch wide **BROWN/PINK GEOMETRIC PRINT** inner border strips.

Step 2 Attach 6-1/2-inch wide **PINK PRINT** outer border strips.

Putting It All Together

Cut the 3-1/2 yard length of backing fabric in half crosswise to make 2, 1-3/4 yard lengths. Refer to *Finishing the Quilt* on page 189 for complete instructions. Our quilt was quilted with an allover quilt design.

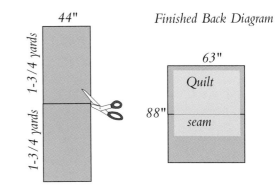

Finished Back Diagram

Binding

Cutting

From **BROWN SOLID**:

• Cut 7, 6-1/2 x 44-inch strips

Sew binding to quilt using a scant 1-inch seam allowance. This measurement will produce a 1-inch wide finished double binding. Refer to **Binding** and **Diagonal Piecing** on page 189 for complete instructions.

Baby Girl Quilt
56-inches square

Daisy Chain

63-inches square

Fabrics & Supplies

1 yard	**GREEN PRINT** for blocks
3/4 yard	**YELLOW PRINT** for block centers, inner border
1-1/4 yards	**BEIGE PRINT** for background
2 yards	**ROSE PRINT** for alternate blocks, outer border
2/3 yard	**YELLOW PRINT** for binding

4 yards for backing

quilt batting, at least 69-inches square

*Before beginning this project,
read through **Getting Started** on page 181.*

9-Patch blocks

Makes 8 blocks

Cutting

From **GREEN PRINT**:
- Cut 4, 3-1/2 x 44-inch strips

From **YELLOW PRINT**:
- Cut 1, 3-1/2 x 44-inch strip

From **BEIGE PRINT**:
- Cut 4, 3-1/2 x 44-inch strips

Piecing

Refer to arrows on diagrams for pressing.

Step 1 Aligning long edges, sew 3-1/2 x 44-inch **GREEN** strips to both side edges of the 3-1/2 x 44-inch **YELLOW** strip. Press strip set referring to ***Hints and Helps for Pressing Strip Sets*** on page 187. Cut strip set into segments.

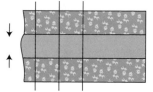

Crosscut 8, 3-1/2-inch wide segments

Step 2 Aligning long edges, sew 3-1/2 x 44-inch **BEIGE** strips to both side edges of a 3-1/2 x 44-inch **GREEN** strip. Make 2 strip sets; press. Cut strip sets into segments.

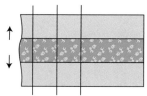

Crosscut 16, 3-1/2-inch wide segments

Step 3 Sew Step 2 segments to top/bottom edges of the Step 1 units; press. <u>At this point each 9-patch block should measure 9-1/2-inches square.</u>

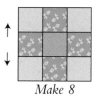

Make 8

Pieced Blocks

Makes 12 blocks

Cutting

From **GREEN PRINT**:
- Cut 3, 3-7/8 x 44-inch strips
- Cut 1, 3-1/2 x 44-inch strip

From **BEIGE PRINT**:
- Cut 3, 3-7/8 x 44-inch strips
- Cut 2, 3-1/2 x 44-inch strips
- Cut 2 more 3-1/2 x 44-inch strips. From strips cut: 24, 3-1/2-inch squares

Piecing

Refer to arrows on diagrams for pressing.

Step 1 Aligning long edges, sew 3-1/2 x 44-inch **BEIGE** strips to both side edges of the 3-1/2 x 44-inch **GREEN** strip; press. Cut strip set into segments.

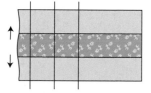

Crosscut 12, 3-1/2-inch wide segments

Step 2 With right sides together, layer the 3-7/8 x 44-inch **GREEN** and **BEIGE** strips in pairs. Press together, but do not sew. Cut the layered strips into squares.

Cut the layered squares in half diagonally to make 48 sets of triangles. Stitch 1/4-inch from the diagonal edge of each pair of triangles; press.

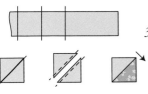

Crosscut 24, 3-7/8-inch squares

Make 48, 3-1/2-inch triangle-pieced squares

Step 3 Sew Step 2 triangle-pieced squares to both side edges of a 3-1/2-inch **BEIGE** square; press.

Make 24

Step 4 Sew Step 3 units to top/bottom edges of the Step 1 segments; press. <u>At this point each pieced block should measure 9-1/2-inches square.</u>

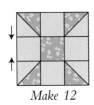

Make 12

Quilt Center

Cutting

From **ROSE PRINT**:
• Cut 2, 9-1/2 x 44-inch strips. From strips cut: 5, 9-1/2-inch alternate block squares

Quilt Center Assembly

Step 1 Referring to quilt center assembly diagram for placement, lay out the 9-patch blocks, pieced blocks, and alternate blocks in 5 rows with 5 blocks in each row.

Step 2 Sew the blocks together in each row. Press seam allowances in alternating directions by rows so the seams will fit snugly together with less bulk. <u>At this point each block row should measure 9-1/2 x 45-1/2-inches.</u>

Step 3 Pin the rows together at the block intersections; stitch and press. <u>At this point the quilt center should measure 45-1/2-inches square.</u>

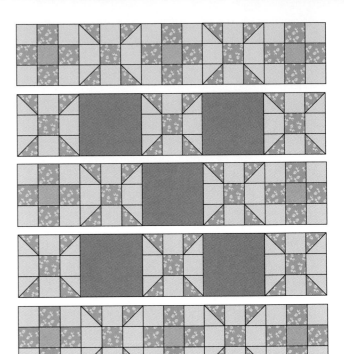

Quilt Center Assembly Diagram

Borders

*Note: Yardage given allows for border strips to be cut on crosswise grain. Diagonally piece strips as needed, referring to **Diagonal Piecing** on page 189. Read through **Border** instructions on page 187 for general instructions on adding borders.*

Cutting

From **YELLOW PRINT**:
• Cut 5, 3-1/2 x 44-inch inner border strips

From **ROSE PRINT**:
• Cut 7, 6-1/2 x 44-inch outer border strips

Attaching the Borders

Press border strips toward borders just added.

Step 1 Attach 3-1/2-inch wide **YELLOW** inner border strips.

Step 2 Attach 6-1/2-inch wide **ROSE** outer border strips.

Putting It All Together

Cut 4 yard length of backing fabric in half crosswise to make 2, 2 yard lengths. Refer to *Finishing the Quilt* on page 189 for complete instructions.

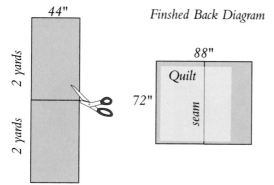

Finshed Back Diagram

Quilting Suggestions:

- **ROSE** alternate blocks –
  TB1 – 9" Loop-d-Loop and in-the-ditch
- Nine-patch blocks – crosshatch

- Pieced blocks - small meander in **BEIGE**
- **YELLOW** inner border –
  TB74 – 2-1/2" Beadwork
- **ROSE** outer border –
  TB111 – 5-1/2" Floral Vine

THIMBLEBERRIES® *quilt stencils by Quilting Creations International are available at your local quilt shop or visit www.quiltingcreations.com.*

Binding

Cutting

From **YELLOW PRINT**:

- Cut 7, 2-3/4 x 44-inch strips

Sew binding to quilt using a 3/8-inch seam allowance. This measurement will produce a 1/2-inch wide finished double binding. Refer to *Binding* and *Diagonal Piecing* on page 189 for complete instructions.

Daisy Chain Baby Quilt
63-inches square

Kids Will Be Kids

48 x 56-inches

Fabrics & Supplies

7/8 yard	**YELLOW PRINT** for blocks, narrow middle border, wide middle border
1/3 yard	**BLUE PRINT** for blocks, inner border
5/8 yard	**RED PRINT** for blocks, checkerboard borders
2/3 yard	**BEIGE PRINT** for side/corner triangles, checkerboard borders
1 yard	**GREEN PRINT** for outer border
5/8 yard	**RED PRINT** for binding

3 yards for backing

quilt batting, at least 54 x 62-inches

Before beginning this project,
*read through **Getting Started** on page 181.*

Pieced Blocks

*Makes 2 **BLUE** and **YELLOW** blocks*
*Makes 6 **RED** and **YELLOW** blocks*

Cutting

From **YELLOW PRINT**:
• Cut 1, 4-1/2 x 44-inch strip. From strip cut:
  8, 4-1/2-inch squares

From **BLUE PRINT**:
• Cut 1, 3-5/8 x 44-inch strip. From strip cut:
  4, 3-5/8-inch squares. Cut the squares in half diagonally to make 8 triangles.

3-5/8" squares

From **RED PRINT**:
• Cut 2, 3-5/8 x 44-inch strips. From strips cut:
  12, 3-5/8-inch squares. Cut the squares in half diagonally to make 24 triangles.

3-5/8" squares

Piecing

Refer to arrows on diagrams for pressing.

Note: *Mark center points along the side edges of each 4-1/2-inch **YELLOW** square. Carefully mark the center points along the **bias** edge of each **BLUE** and **RED** triangle. <u>Be careful not to stretch the bias edges.</u>*

Bias edge

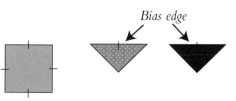

Step 1 With right sides together and raw edges even, center a **BLUE** triangle at the top edge of a 4-1/2-inch **YELLOW** square. Pin the layers together being careful not to stretch the **bias** edges; stitch and press. In the same manner, stitch a **BLUE** triangle to the bottom edge of the **YELLOW** square; press. Stitch

BLUE triangles to the remaining side edges of the square; press. <u>At this point each pieced block should measure 6-1/8-inches square.</u>

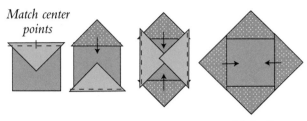

Match center points

Make 2

Step 2 With right sides together, center, pin, and stitch a **RED** triangle to the top edge of a 4-1/2-inch **YELLOW** square; press. In the same manner, stitch a **RED** triangle to the bottom edge of the **YELLOW** square; press. Stitch **RED** triangles to the remaining side edges of the square; press. <u>At this point each pieced block should measure 6-1/8-inches square.</u>

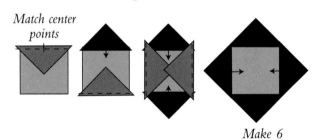

Match center points

Make 6

Quilt Center

Note: Side and corner triangles are larger than necessary and will be trimmed before borders are added.

Cutting

From **BEIGE PRINT**:
• Cut 1, 9-1/2 x 44-inch strip. From strip cut:
   2, 9-1/2-inch squares. Cut squares diagonally into quarters for a total of 8 triangles.

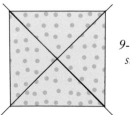

9-1/2" squares side triangles

You will be using 6 for side triangles.

• Cut 2, 5-1/2-inch squares. Cut the squares in half diagonally for a total of 4 corner triangles.

5-1/2" squares corner triangles

Quilt Center Assembly

Step 1 Referring to quilt center assembly diagram for block placement, sew pieced blocks, **BEIGE** side triangles, and **BEIGE** corner triangles together in diagonal rows. Press seam allowances in alternating directions by rows so the seams will fit snugly together with less bulk.

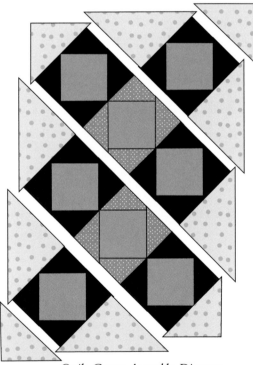

Quilt Center Assembly Diagram

Step 2 Trim away excess fabric from side/corner triangles, taking care to allow a 1/4-inch seam allowance beyond the corners of each block. Refer to **Trimming Side and Corner Triangles** for complete instructions. <u>At this point the quilt center should measure 16-1/2 x 24-1/2-inches.</u>

Trimming Side and Corner Triangles

Begin at a corner by lining up your ruler 1/4-inch beyond the points of the block corners as shown. Cut along the edge of the ruler. Repeat this procedure on all four sides of the quilt top.

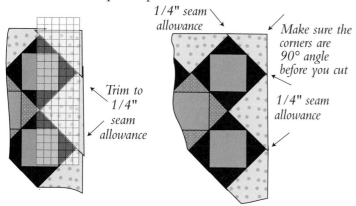

Borders

*Note: Yardage given allows for border strips to be cut on crosswise grain. Diagonally piece strips as needed, referring to **Diagonal Piecing** instructions on page 189. Read through **Border** instructions on page 187 for general instructions on adding borders.*

Cutting

From **BLUE PRINT**:
• Cut 3, 1-1/2 x 44-inch inner border strips

From **YELLOW PRINT**:
• Cut 4, 4-1/2 x 44-inch wide middle border strips
• Cut 3, 1-1/2 x 44-inch narrow middle border strips

From **RED PRINT**:
• Cut 4, 2-1/2 x 44-inch strips

From **BEIGE PRINT**:
• Cut 4, 2-1/2 x 44-inch strips

From **GREEN PRINT**:
• Cut 5, 6-1/2 x 44-inch outer border strips

Attaching Borders

Press seam allowances toward borders just added.

Step 1 Attach 1-1/2-inch wide **BLUE** inner border strips.

Step 2 Attach 1-1/2-inch wide **YELLOW** narrow middle border strips.

Step 3 Aligning long edges, sew 2-1/2 x 44-inch **RED** and **BEIGE** strips together in pairs. Press seam allowances toward darker fabric referring to *Hints and Helps for Pressing Strip Sets* on page 187. Make a total of 4 strip sets. Cut strip sets into segments.

Crosscut 64, 2-1/2-inch wide segments

Step 4 For top/bottom checkerboard borders, sew 5 segments together; press. Sew the borders to the top/bottom edges of the quilt center; press.

Make 2 for top/bottom borders

Step 5 For side checkerboard borders, sew 8 segments together; press. Sew the borders to the side edges of the quilt center; press.

Make 2 for side borders

Step 6 Attach 4-1/2-inch wide **YELLOW** wide middle border strips.

Step 7 For top/bottom checkerboard borders, sew 8 segments together; press. Sew the borders to the top/bottom edges of the quilt center; press.

Make 2 for top/bottom borders

Step 8 For side checkerboard borders, sew 11 segments together; press. Sew the borders to the side edges of the quilt center; press.

Make 2 for side borders

Step 9 Attach 6-1/2-inch wide **GREEN** outer border strips.

Putting It All Together

Cut 3 yard length of backing fabric in half crosswise to make 2, 1-1/2 yard lengths. Refer to *Finishing the Quilt* on page 189 for complete instructions.

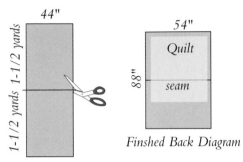

Finshed Back Diagram

Quilting Suggestions:

• Blocks – **TB119 – 5" Petal Square** (on-point)

• **BEIGE** side triangles –
  1/2 of **TB120 – 7-1/2" Petal Square**

• **BEIGE** corner triangles –
  1/2 of **TB118 – 3-1/2" Petal Square**

TB119-5" Petal Square
TB120-7-1/2" Petal Square
TB118-3-1/2" Petal Square

• **BLUE/YELLOW** narrow borders – in-the-ditch

• Checkerboard borders – in-the-ditch and big X in **BEIGE** squares

• **YELLOW** wide middle border –
  TB116 – 3-1/2" Leaf Wave

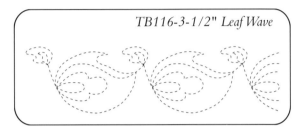

TB116-3-1/2" Leaf Wave

• **GREEN** outer border – meander

THIMBLEBERRIES® *quilt stencils by Quilting Creations International are available at your local quilt shop or visit www.quiltingcreations.com.*

Binding

Cutting

From **RED PRINT**:

• Cut 6, 2-3/4 x 44-inch strips

Sew binding to quilt using a 3/8-inch seam allowance. This measurement will produce a 1/2-inch wide finished double binding. Refer to *Binding* and *Diagonal Piecing* on page 189 for complete instructions.

Kids Will Be Kids Quilt

48 x 56-inches

Chunky Chunk with Ruffle

36 x 48-inches

Fabrics & Supplies

1/2 yard **BLUE/PURPLE FLORAL** for quilt center

1/2 yard **LIGHT GREEN PRINT** for quilt center

3/8 yard **PINK PRINT** for quilt center

1/3 yard **SMALL BLUE/PURPLE PRINT** for quilt center

2 yards **DARK PURPLE FLORAL** for sawtooth unit, ruffle

1/4 yard **BEIGE PRINT** for sawtooth units

1/4 yard **YELLOW PRINT** for inner border

5/8 yard **AQUA PRINT** for outer border

2 yards **BRIGHT PINK PRINT** for facing and backing

quilt batting, at least 42 x 54-inches

*Before beginning this project, read through **Getting Started** on page 181.*

Block A

Makes 8 blocks

Cutting

From **BLUE/PURPLE FLORAL**:
• Cut 2, 7-1/2 x 44-inch strips. From strips cut:
    8, 7-1/2 x 10-1/2-inch rectangles

From **LIGHT GREEN PRINT**:
• Cut 3, 5-1/2 x 44-inch strips. From strips cut:
    16, 5-1/2-inch squares

Piecing

Refer to arrows on diagrams for pressing.

With right sides together, position a 5-1/2-inch **LIGHT GREEN** square on the corner of a 7-1/2 x 10-1/2-inch **BLUE/PURPLE FLORAL** rectangle. Draw a diagonal line on the square; stitch on the line. Trim seam allowance to 1/4-inch; press. Repeat this process at the opposite corner of the rectangle; press.

 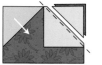

Make 8
Block A

Block B

Makes 8 blocks

Cutting

From **PINK PRINT**:
• Cut 2, 3-1/2 x 44-inch strips.

***Note:** If your fabric is not 44-inches long you will need to cut another 3-1/2 x 44-inch strip. Cut this strip in half to make 2, 3-1/2 x 22-inch strips to make a partial strip set.*

From **SMALL BLUE/PURPLE PRINT**:
• Cut 1, 4-1/2 x 44-inch strip.

***Note:** If your fabric is not 44-inches long you will need to cut a 4-1/2 x 22-inch strip to make a partial strip set.*

Piecing

Refer to arrows on diagrams for pressing.

Aligning long raw edges, sew a 3-1/2 x 44-inch **PINK** strip to the top/bottom edges of a 4-1/2 x 44-inch **SMALL BLUE/PURPLE PRINT** strip. Press referring to ***Hints and***

Helps for Pressing Strip Sets on page 187. Cut strip sets into segments. Make a partial strip set if needed.

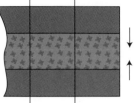

Crosscut 8, 5-1/2-inch wide segments

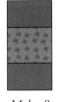

Make 8 Block B

Sawtooth Units

Makes 8 units

Cutting

From **DARK PURPLE FLORAL**:

• Cut 2, 2-7/8 x 44-inch strips

From **BEIGE PRINT**:

• Cut 2, 2-7/8 x 44-inch strips

Piecing

Refer to arrows on diagrams for pressing.

Step 1 With right sides together, layer 2-7/8 x 44-inch **DARK PURPLE FLORAL** and **BEIGE** strips together in pairs. Press together, but do not sew. Cut layered strips into squares. Cut layered squares in half diagonally to make 40 sets of triangles. Stitch 1/4-inch from diagonal edge of each triangle set; press.

Crosscut 20, 2-7/8-inch squares

Make 40, 2-1/2-inch triangle-pieced squares

Step 2 Sew 5 triangle-pieced squares together for each sawtooth unit; press. At this point each sawtooth unit should measure 2-1/2 x 10-1/2-inches.

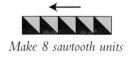

Make 8 sawtooth units

Step 3 Sew each sawtooth unit to right edge of each Block B; press. At this point each Block B/sawtooth unit should measure 7-1/2 x 10-1/2-inches.

Make 8

Step 4 Referring to quilt photograph on page 127, sew blocks together in 4 rows with 4 blocks in each row. Press seam allowances in alternating directions by rows so seam allowances will fit snugly together with less bulk. Sew rows together; press. At this point the quilt center should measure 28-1/2 x 40-1/2-inches.

Borders

Note: *Yardage given allows for border strips to be cut on crosswise grain. Diagonally piece strips as needed referring to **Diagonal Piecing** instructions on page 189. Read through **Border** instructions on page 187 for general instructions on adding borders.*

Cutting

From **YELLOW PRINT**:

• Cut 4, 1-1/2 x 44-inch inner border strips

From **AQUA PRINT**:

• Cut 5, 3-1/2 x 44-inch outer border strips

Attaching the Borders

Press seam allowances toward borders just added.

Step 1 Attach 1-1/2-inch wide **YELLOW** inner border strips.

Step 2 Attach 3-1/2-inch wide **AQUA** outer border strips.

Putting It All Together

Cutting

From **BRIGHT PINK PRINT**:

- Cut 1, 42 x 54-inch backing rectangle.
  From the remaining fabric cut enough 2-3/4-inch wide **bias** strips to make a 175-inch long facing strip. Diagonally piece the facing strips together. Fold the strip in half lengthwise, wrong sides together; press. Unfold and trim one end at a 45° angle. Turn under the edge 1/4-inch; press. Refold the strip.

From **DARK PURPLE FLORAL**:

- Cut 11, 5 x 44-inch strips for the ruffle. Diagonally piece the strips together to make a continuous ruffle strip. Fold the strip in half lengthwise, wrong sides together; press. Divide ruffle strip into 4 equal segments; mark quarter points with safety pins.

Quilting

Step 1 Trim batting and backing so they are approximately 6-inches larger than quilt top. Refer to **Finishing the Quilt** on page 189 for complete instructions. Our quilt was quilted with an allover floral design.

Step 2 Referring to the cutting guide for curved corners on page 126, round off the 4 corners.

Ruffle and Facing

Step 1 To gather ruffle, position a heavy thread (quilting thread) 1/4-inch in from raw edges of ruffle strip. Thread should be about 340-inches long. Secure one end by stitching across it. Zigzag stitch over the thread all the way around ruffle strip taking care not to sew through the thread.

Step 2 Divide the quilt edges into 4 equal segments; mark quarter points. With right sides together and raw edges aligned, pin ruffle to quilt matching quarter points. Gently pull on gathering stitches until ruffle fits quilt top taking care to allow extra fullness in the ruffle at each corner. Sew ruffle to quilt using a 1/4-inch seam allowance.

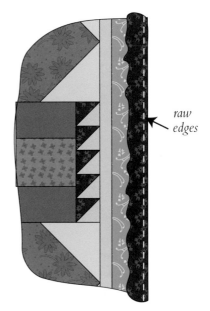

Step 3 With raw edges even, lay the prepared **BRIGHT PINK** facing strip on the right side of the quilt with the ruffle sandwiched between the layers and turned in toward the center of the quilt at this time. Stitch the facing in place with a 1/2-inch seam allowance.

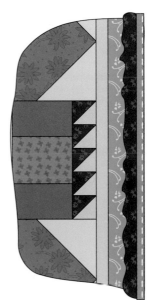

Step 4 To eliminate some of the bulk, grade the seam allowances as needed. Turn the facing to the back side of the quilt so the ruffle lays out flat. Hand sew the facing in place.

Quilt Back

Facing

Cutting Guide for Curved Corners

Chunky Chunk Baby Quilt with Ruffle

36 x 48-inches

Baby Boy

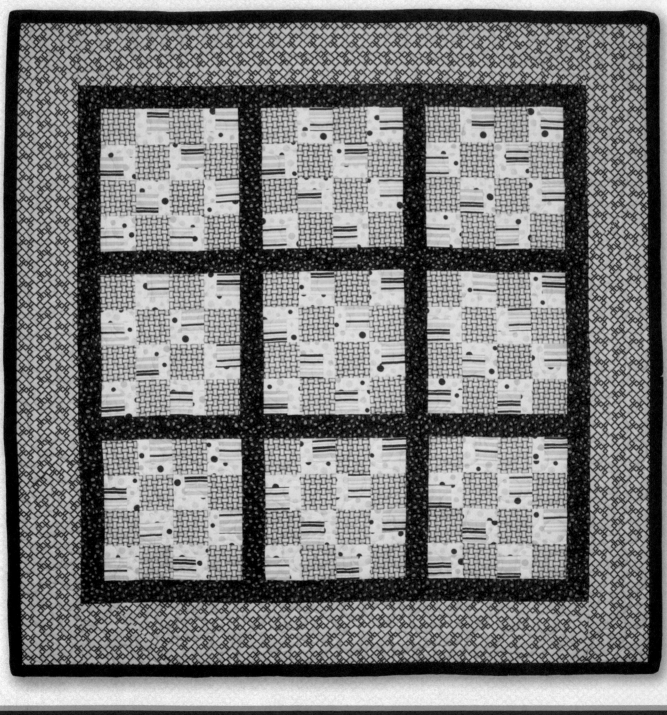

56-inches square

Fabrics & Supplies

1/2 yard **BLUE/BROWN STRIPE** for blocks

5/8 yard **BLUE/BROWN DOT** for blocks

7/8 yard **BLUE/BROWN WEAVE PRINT** for blocks

3/4 yard **BROWN PRINT** for lattice, inner border

1-1/4 yards **BLUE/BROWN GEOMETRIC PRINT** for outer border

1-1/3 yards **BROWN SOLID** for wide binding

3-1/2 yards for backing

quilt batting, at least 62-inches square

*Before beginning this project, read through **Getting Started** on page 181.*

Pieced Blocks

Makes 9 blocks

Cutting

From **BLUE/BROWN STRIPE**:
• Cut 5, 2-1/2 x 44-inch strips

From **BLUE/BROWN DOT**:
• Cut 3, 3-1/2 x 44-inch strips. From strips cut:
72, 1-1/2 x 3-1/2-inch rectangles
• Cut 5, 1-1/2 x 44-inch strips

From **BLUE/BROWN WEAVE PRINT**:
• Cut 7, 3-1/2 x 44-inch strips. From strips cut:
72, 3-1/2-inch squares

Piecing

Refer to arrows on diagrams for pressing.

Step 1 Aligning long edges, sew together the 1-1/2 x 44-inch **BLUE/BROWN DOT** strips and the 2-1/2 x 44-inch **BLUE/BROWN STRIPE** strips in pairs; press. Make 5 strip sets. Cut the strip sets into segments. Sew a 1-1/2 x 3-1/2-inch **BLUE/BROWN DOT** rectangle to the right edge of each unit; press. <u>At this point each unit should measure 3-1/2-inches square.</u>

Crosscut 72, 2-1/2-inch wide segments

Make 72

Step 2 Referring to the block diagram, sew together 8 Step 1 units and 8, 3-1/2-inch **BLUE/BROWN WEAVE PRINT** squares in 4 rows; press. Sew the rows together; press. <u>At this point each block should measure 12-1/2-inches square.</u>

Note: *Pay close attention to the Step 1 block placement.*

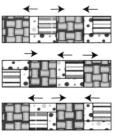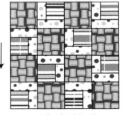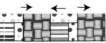

Make 9 blocks

Quilt Center

Cutting

From **BROWN PRINT**:

• Cut 4, 2-1/2 x 44-inch strips. From strips cut:
2, 2-1/2 x 40-1/2-inch lattice strips
6, 2-1/2 x 12-1/2-inch lattice segments

Quilt Center Assembly

Step 1 Referring to quilt illustration on page 131, sew together 3 of the pieced blocks and 2 of the 2-1/2 x 12-1/2-inch **BROWN** lattice segments; press. Make 3 block rows. <u>At this point each block row should measure 12-1/2 x 40-1/2-inches.</u>

Step 2 Sew together the block rows and the 2-1/2 x 40-1/2-inch **BROWN** lattice strips; press. <u>At this point the quilt center should measure 40-1/2-inches square.</u>

Borders

*Note: Yardage given allows for border strips to be cut on crosswise grain. Diagonally piece the strips as needed, referring to **Diagonal Piecing** instructions on page 189. Read through **Border** instructions on page 187 for general instructions on adding borders.*

Cutting

From **BROWN PRINT**:

• Cut 5, 2-1/2 x 44-inch inner border strips

From **BLUE/BROWN GEOMETRIC PRINT**:

• Cut 6, 6-1/2 x 44-inch outer border strips

Attaching Borders

Step 1 Attach 2-1/2-inch wide **BROWN** inner border strips.

Step 2 Attach 6-1/2-inch wide **BLUE/BROWN GEOMETRIC PRINT** outer border strips.

Putting It All Together

Cut the 3-1/2 yard length of backing fabric in half crosswise to make 2, 1-3/4 yard lengths. Refer to *Finishing the Quilt* on page 189 for complete instructions. Our quilt was quilted with an allover design.

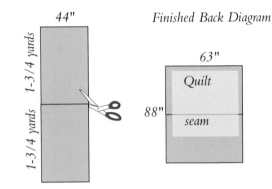

Binding

Cutting

From **BROWN SOLID**:

• Cut 7, 6-1/2 x 44-inch strips

Sew binding to quilt using a scant 1-inch seam allowance. This measurement will produce a 1-inch wide finished double binding. Refer to *Binding* and *Diagonal Piecing* on page 189 for complete instructions.

Baby Boy Quilt
56-inches square

pillows

Lazy Daisy

18-inches square without ruffle

Fabrics & Supplies

20-inch square **BEIGE PRINT** for center square

5/8 yard **GREEN STRIPE** for outer ruffle

1-1/4 yards **ROSE FLORAL** for inner ruffle, pillow back

template material: manila folder, plastic

18-1/2-inch freezer paper square for stabilizer

mechanical pencil for tracing

Crayola® crayons, paper towels

embroidery floss for decorative stitches: black

22-inch square of **BEIGE** for pillow top lining

22-inch square of quilt batting

18-inch square pillow form

(9) 1/4-inch black ball buttons

matching thread for quilting:
Sulky® "Flying Colors",
Ecru 733-1082

*Before beginning this project, read through **Getting Started** on page 181.*

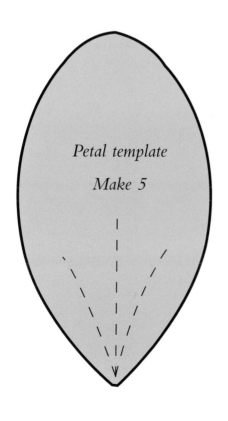

Petal template

Make 5

Pillow Top

Cutting

From **BEIGE PRINT**:
- Cut 1, 20-inch pillow top square. The square will be trimmed to 18-1/2-inches when the coloring and embroidery are complete.

From **BEIGE** lining and batting:
- Cut 1, 22-inch square from each

From freezer paper:
- Cut 1, 18-inch square

Coloring and Embroidering the Pillow Top

Step 1 Fuse freezer paper square to wrong side of 20-inch **BEIGE PRINT** pillow top square. The freezer paper will stabilize the fabric making it easier to draw on.

Step 2 Make 5 petal templates. Referring to the photograph, position the petal templates on the 20-inch **BEIGE** square to make a flower. Our pillow shows the 3 flowers are within a 15-inch square. Using a mechanical pencil, lightly trace the petal shapes onto the **BEIGE** pillow top to make 3 flowers.

Step 3 Using crayons, color the petals as desired. Lay colored fabric face down on 2 layers of paper toweling and press with a dry iron for 5 seconds. This will release the wax and set the color. Remove freezer paper. With 3 strands of black embroidery floss, outline stitch the petals.

Outline Stitch

Quilt Pillow Top

Step 1 Layer 22-inch **BEIGE** lining square, batting, and pillow top facing up. Baste layers together; quilt as desired.

Step 2 Our project was quilted with the echo design around the flowers and 3 veins were quilted in each petal. Trim pillow top unit to 18-1/2-inches square.

Step 3 Hand baste edges together to prevent them from rippling when the ruffle is attached. Sew 3 buttons to each flower center.

Pillow Ruffle

Note: By sewing 2 different fabric widths together, you form the illusion of a double ruffle without additional bulk.

Cutting

From **ROSE FLORAL**:

• Cut 5, 2-5/8 x 44-inch strips for inner ruffle

From **GREEN STRIPE**:

• Cut 5, 3-5/8 x 44-inch strips for outer ruffle

Piecing and Attaching the Ruffle

Step 1 Piece the 2-5/8-inch wide **ROSE FLORAL** strips together; press. Piece the 3-5/8-inch wide **GREEN STRIPE** strips together; press.

Step 2 Aligning long raw edges, sew the **ROSE FLORAL** and **GREEN STRIPE** strips together; press. With right sides facing, sew short raw edges together to make a continuous circle; press.

Step 3 Fold the strip in half lengthwise, wrong sides together; press. Divide ruffle strip into 4 equal segments; mark quarter points with safety pins. Mark quarter points on pillow top.

Step 4 To gather ruffle, position a heavyweight thread 1/4-inch from raw edge of folded ruffle strip. You will need a length of thread 144-inches long. Secure one end of the heavy thread by stitching across it. Zigzag stitch over the thread all the way around the ruffle strip, taking care not to sew through the thread.

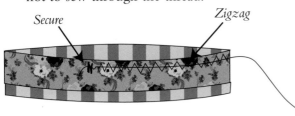

Secure   *Zigzag*

Step 5 With right sides together and raw edges aligned, pin ruffle to pillow top matching quarter points of ruffle and pillow; pin in place.

Step 6 Gently pull gathering stitches until ruffle fits pillow top, taking care to allow a little extra ruffle at each corner for a full look. Pin in place and machine baste ruffle to pillow top using a 1/4-inch seam allowance.

Pillow Back

Cutting

From **ROSE FLORAL**:

• Cut 2, 18-1/2 x 26-inch rectangles

Assemble Pillow Back

Step 1 With wrong sides together, fold the 18-1/2 x 26-inch rectangles in half to make 2, 13 x 18-1/2-inch double-thick pillow back pieces. Overlap the 2 folded edges so the pillow back measures 18-1/2-inches square; pin. Stitch around entire pillow back to create a single pillow back.

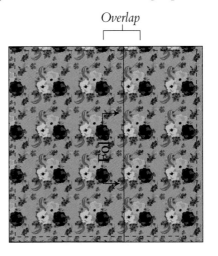

Overlap

Step 2 With right sides together, layer pillow back and pillow top; pin. The ruffle will be sandwiched between the 2 layers and turned in toward the pillow center. Stitch around the outside edge using a 3/8-inch seam allowance.

Step 3 Turn pillow right side out and fluff up ruffle. Insert pillow form through back opening.

pillows

In The Pines

18-inches square

Fabrics & Supplies

5/8 yard	**BEIGE PRINT** for appliqué foundation, quilted pillow top lining
1 yard	**BROWN/RED FLORAL** for upper section of pillow top, pillow back
1/8 yard	**RED PRINT** for ruffle
1/4 yard	**GREEN PRINT** for tree appliqués

22-inch square quilt batting for quilted pillow top

18-inch pillow form

paper-backed fusible web

tear-away fabric stabilizer

template material

machine embroidery thread or pearl cotton for decorative stitches: black

(5) 1-1/8-inch diameter buttons

spray adhesive for basting (optional)

*Before beginning this project,
read through **Getting Started** on page 181.*

Pillow Top

Cutting

From **BEIGE PRINT**:
• Cut 1, 22-inch pillow lining square.
    Set this square aside to be used in the **Pillow Assembly** section.
• Cut 1, 14 x 19-1/2-inch rectangle.
    This rectangle is larger than necessary and will be trimmed to 12-5/8 x 18-1/2-inches when the appliqué is complete. The **BEIGE** rectangle may shrink up a bit during the appliqué process, therefore a bit extra fabric is allowed.

From **BROWN/RED FLORAL**:
• Cut 1, 6-5/8 x 18-1/2-inch rectangle

Paper-Backed Fusible Web Appliqué

Step 1 Make a template using the tree shape on page 139. Trace the shape on the paper side of the fusible web, leaving a small margin between each shape. Cut the shapes apart.

Step 2 When you are fusing a large shape like the tree, fuse just the outer edges of the shape so the center is softer to the touch and it will not look stiff when finished. Cut away fusible web about 3/8-inch inside the shape.

Step 3 Following the manufacturer's instructions, fuse the shapes to the wrong side of the fabric chosen for the appliqués. Let the fabric cool and cut along the traced line. Peel away the paper backing from the fusible web.

Step 4 Referring to the pillow photograph, position the appliqué shapes on the 14 x 19-1/2-inch **BEIGE** appliqué foundation rectangle. The trees are placed about 3-1/4-inches from the bottom edge (19-1/2-inch side) of the **BEIGE** rectangle and the lower boughs are about 1/8-inch apart. Fuse the shapes in place.

Step 5 For machine appliqué, we suggest pinning a square of tear-away stabilizer to the back side of the **BEIGE** rectangle so it will lay flat when the appliqué is complete. We machine blanket stitched around shapes using black embroidery thread for the top thread and regular sewing thread in the bobbin. If you like, you could hand blanket stitch around shapes with pearl cotton.

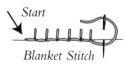

Start

Blanket Stitch

Note: *To prevent hand blanket stitches from "rolling off" edges of appliqué shapes, take an extra backstitch in the same place as you made the blanket stitch, going around outer curves, corners, and points. For straight edges, taking a backstitch every inch is enough.*

Step 6 When the appliqué is complete, trim the **BEIGE** rectangle to 12-5/8 x 18-1/2-inches.

Note: The bottom edge of the trees should be 2-3/4-inches from the bottom edge of the BEIGE rectangle at this time.

Ruffle

Cutting

From **RED PRINT**:

• Cut 1, 2-3/4 x 44-inch strip for the ruffle

Attaching the Ruffle

Step 1 Fold the 2-3/4-inch wide **RED** strip in half lengthwise, wrong sides together; press. Mark the center point of the ruffle strip with a safety pin.

Step 2 To gather the ruffle, machine baste 3 lines of stitching close together. Place the stitches 1/8-inch, a scant 1/4-inch, and 3/8-inch from the raw edges. With this gathering method the gathers of the narrow ruffle are held in place nicely.

Step 3 Divide the upper edge (18-1/2-inch side) of the **BEIGE** rectangle in half and mark. With raw edges aligned and center points matching, pin the prepared ruffle to the upper edge of the **BEIGE** rectangle. Pull up the gathering stitches until the ruffle fits the pillow front. Machine baste the ruffle in place using a scant 1/4-inch seam allowance. (The basting stitches that show will be removed in Step 4.)

Step 4 With right sides together, position the 6-5/8 x 18-1/2-inch **BROWN/RED FLORAL** rectangle at the upper edge of the **BEIGE** rectangle. The ruffle will be sandwiched between the 2 layers. Pin and stitch the pieces together using a 3/8-inch seam allowance. Press seam allowances toward the **BROWN/RED FLORAL** rectangle.

Remove any gathering stitches that show. At this point the pillow top should measure 18-1/2-inches square.

Pillow Top Assembly

Basting Suggestions: We suggest using spray adhesive for basting (follow manufacturer's instructions); or hand baste the layers together.

Step 1 Layer the 22-inch square **BEIGE** lining (cut previously), batting, and pieced pillow top. Hand or spray baste the layers together and quilt as desired. When quilting is complete, trim the excess **BEIGE** lining and batting even with the pillow top (18-1/2-inches square).

Step 2 Hand baste the edges together. This will prevent the edge of the pillow top from rippling when it is sewn to the backing.

Step 3 Referring to the pillow photograph on page 136, sew the buttons to the pillow top.

Pillow Back

Cutting

From **BROWN/RED FLORAL**:

• Cut 1, 24 x 44-inch strip. From strip cut:
  2, 18-1/2 x 24-inch pillow back rectangles

Pillow Back Assembly

Step 1 With wrong sides together, fold each **BROWN/RED FLORAL** pillow back rectangle in half crosswise to make 2, 12 x 18-1/2-inch double-thick pillow back pieces. Overlap the 2 folded edges so the pillow back measures 18-1/2-inches square. Pin the pieces together and machine baste around the entire piece to create a single pillow back, using a 1/4-inch seam allowance. The double thickness of the pillow back will make it more stable and give it a nice finishing touch.

Step 2 With right sides together, layer the pillow back and the pillow top; pin. Stitch around the outside edges using a 3/8-inch seam allowance.

Turn the pillow right side out and insert the pillow form through the back opening.

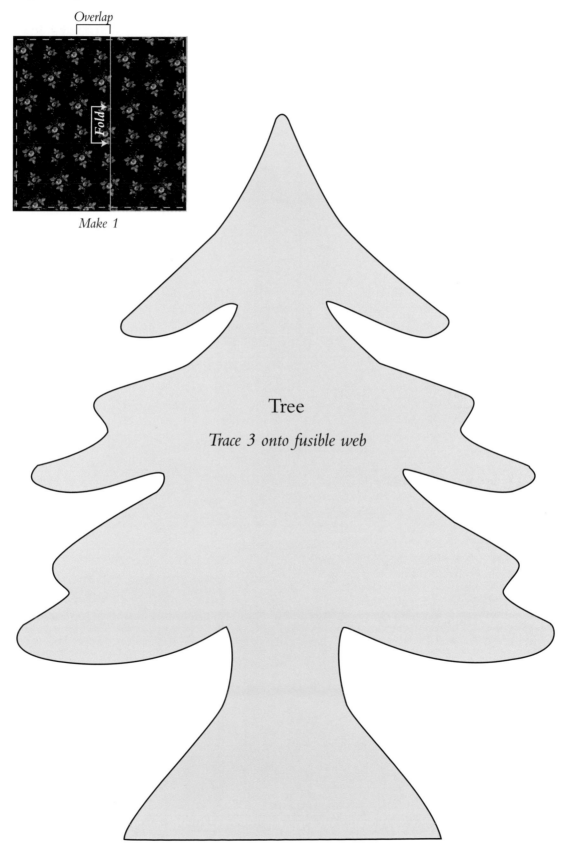

Overlap

Fold

Make 1

Tree

Trace 3 onto fusible web

Big Patch

18-inches square

Fabrics & Supplies

1-1/8 yards	**LARGE BROWN FLORAL** for pillow top, pillow back
11-inch square	**GREEN FLORAL** for pillow top
11-inch square	**BROWN PRINT** for appliqué foundation
5 x 8-inch piece	**RUST PRINT** for large leaf appliqué
4 x 7-inch piece	**GREEN PRINT** for small leaf appliqué
3-inch square	**GOLD PRINT** for berry appliqué
1/4 yard	**BROWN DIAGONAL PRINT** for binding

18-inch pillow form

machine-embroidery thread or pearl cotton for
 decorative stitches: black, gold

paper-backed fusible web for appliqués

template material

tear away fabric stabilizer

*Before beginning this project,
read through **Getting Started** on page 181.*

Pillow Top

Cutting

From **LARGE BROWN FLORAL**:
- Cut 1, 8-1/2 x 19-inch rectangle
- Cut 1, 8-1/2 x 11-inch rectangle

From **GREEN FLORAL**:
- Cut 1, 11-inch square

Piecing

Sew together the 8-1/2 x 11-inch **LARGE BROWN FLORAL** rectangle, the 11-inch **GREEN FLORAL** square and the 8-1/2 x 19-inch large **BROWN FLORAL** rectangle; press. At this point the pillow top should measure 19-inches square.

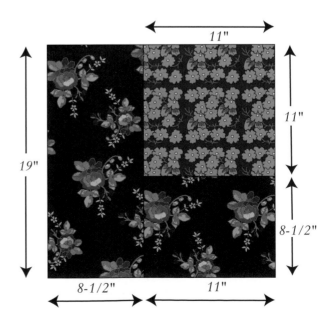

Paper-Backed Fusible Web Appliqué

Step 1 Make templates using the shapes on page 143. Trace the shapes on paper side of the fusible web.

Step 2 When you are fusing a large shape like the leaf, fuse just the outer edges of the shape so the center is softer to the touch and it will not look stiff when finished. Cut away fusible web about 3/8-inch inside the shape.

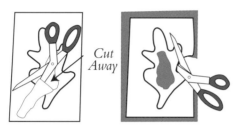

Step 3 Following manufacturer's instructions, fuse shapes to wrong side of fabrics chosen for appliqués. Let fabric cool and cut along traced line. Peel away paper backing from fusible web.

Step 4 Referring to the placement diagram, center the prepared 8 x 9-inch **BROWN PRINT** appliqué foundation rectangle on the pillow top; fuse in place.

Step 5 For machine appliqué, we suggest pinning a square of tear-away stabilizer to the backside of the pillow top so it will lay flat when the machine appliqué is complete. Use the blanket stitch and machine embroidery thread to secure the shapes in place. When the appliqué is complete, tear away the stabilizer. Our sample was hand blanket stitched using pearl cotton.

Blanket Stitch

Note: *To prevent hand blanket stitches from "rolling off" the edges of the appliqué shapes, take an extra backstitch in the same place as you made the blanket stitch, going around outer curves, corners, and points. For straight edges, taking a backstitch every inch is enough.*

Step 6 Referring to the placement diagram, position the remaining shapes on the appliqué foundation square; fuse in place. Either machine blanket stitch or hand blanket stitch

around the shapes using black embroidery thread/pearl cotton.

Placement Diagram

Pillow Back

Cutting

From **LARGE BROWN FLORAL**:

• Cut 2, 19 x 25-inch pillow back rectangles

Assembling the Pillow Back

Step 1 With wrong sides together, fold each 19 x 25-inch **LARGE BROWN FLORAL** pillow back rectangle in half crosswise to make 2, 12-1/2 x 19-inch double-thick pillow back pieces. Overlap the 2 folded edges so the pillow back measures 19-inches square. Pin the pieces together and stitch a 1/4-inch seam allowance around the entire piece to create a single pillow back.

Step 2 With **wrong** sides together, layer pillow back and pillow top; pin. Stitch around outside edges using a scant 1/2-inch seam allowance.

Binding

Cutting

From **BROWN DIAGONAL PRINT**:

• Cut 2, 3-1/2 x 44-inch strips

Sew binding to pillow using a 1/2-inch seam allowance. Refer to **Binding** and **Diagonal Piecing** on page 189 for complete instructions. Insert pillow form through back opening.

Appliqué Pieces

The appliqué shapes are reversed for tracing purposes. When the appliqué is finished it will appear as in the illustration.

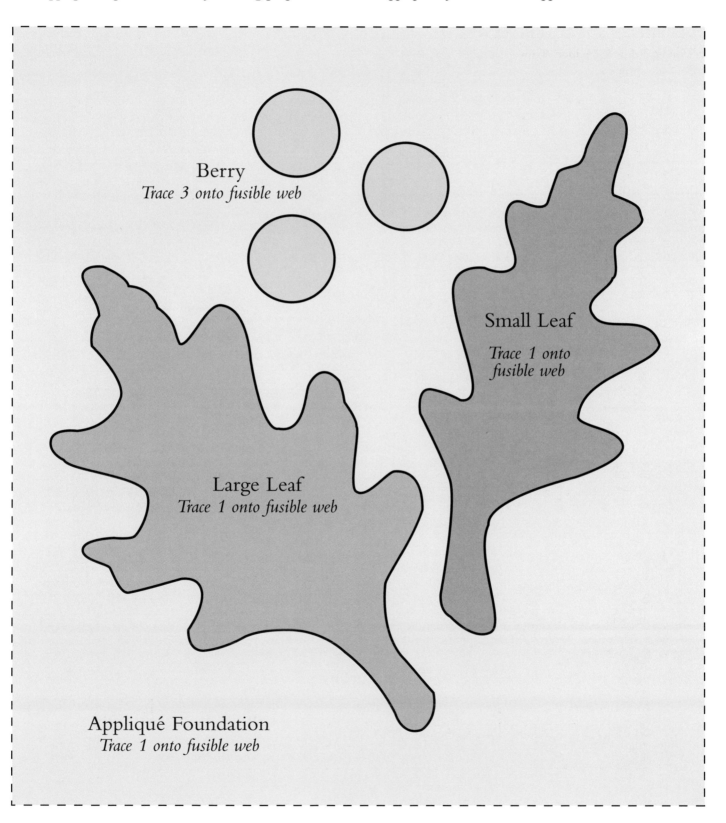

Berry
Trace 3 onto fusible web

Small Leaf

*Trace 1 onto
fusible web*

Large Leaf
Trace 1 onto fusible web

Appliqué Foundation
Trace 1 onto fusible web

In Full Bloom

20 x 26-inches

Fabrics & Supplies

1/2 yard **LARGE GREEN FLORAL** for pillow top (approximately 16-1/2-inches square)

1-3/8 yards **RUST PRINT** for inner borders, pillow back, inner pillow

1/2 yard **GOLD FLORAL** for outer borders

22-inch square **BEIGE** for pillow top lining

22-inch square quilt batting for pillow top

20 x 26-inch standard pillow form

Before beginning this project, read through **Getting Started** *on page 181.*

Inner Pillow

Cutting

From **RUST PRINT**:

- Cut 1, 26-1/2 x 44-inch strip. From strip cut: 2, 20-1/2 x 26-1/2-inch rectangles for inner pillow cover

Piecing

Step 1 With right sides facing, sew together 20-1/2 x 26-1/2-inch **RUST** rectangles leaving a 9-inch opening on one side for turning.

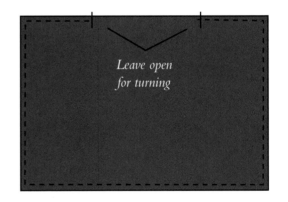

Leave open for turning

Step 2 Turn pillow case right side out, insert pillow form, and sew opening closed.

Pillow Sham

Cutting

From **LARGE GREEN FLORAL**:

- Cut 1, 17-1/2-inch square for pillow top.

From **BEIGE** lining and batting:

- Cut 1, 22-inch square from each

Quilt Pillow Top Square

Step 1 Layer 22-inch **BEIGE** lining square, batting square, and 17-1/2-inch **LARGE GREEN FLORAL** square facing up.

Step 2 Pin or hand baste layers together and quilt by hand or machine. Our sample was quilted with a meandering design. <u>Trim the quilted pillow top unit to 16-1/2-inches square.</u>

Step 3 Hand baste the edges together to prevent them from rippling when the border is sewn to the quilted square.

Borders and Backing

Cutting

From **RUST PRINT**:

• Cut 1, 20-1/2 x 44-inch strip. From strip cut:
    1, 20-1/2-inch square for pillow back
    2, 2-1/2 x 20-1/2-inch side border strips
    2, 2-1/2 x 16-1/2-inch top/bottom border strips

From **GOLD FLORAL**:

• Cut 2, 6-1/2 x 44-inch strips. From strips cut:
    4, 6-1/2 x 20-1/2-inch side outer border strips for pillow top/pillow back

Piecing

Step 1 With right sides together, sew 2-1/2 x 16-1/2-inch **RUST** border strips to the top/bottom edges of the 16-1/2-inch quilted square; press. Sew 2-1/2 x 20-1/2-inch **RUST** border strips to side edges of the quilted square; press. <u>At this point the pillow top should measure 20-1/2-inches square.</u>

Step 2 Fold the 6-1/2 x 20-1/2-inch **GOLD FLORAL** border strips in half lengthwise with wrong sides together; press. With right sides together and raw edges aligned, sew the folded strips to the side edges of the pillow top; press. <u>At this point the pillow sham top should measure 20-1/2 x 26-inches.</u>

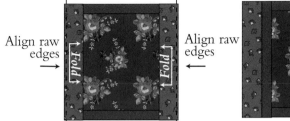

Align raw edges →   ← Align raw edges

Step 3 In the same manner, fold and sew the remaining 6-1/2 x 20-1/2-inch **GOLD FLORAL** border strips to side edges of the 20-1/2-inch **RUST** pillow back square; press. <u>At this point the pillow sham back should measure 20-1/2 x 26-inches.</u>

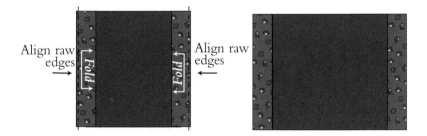

Align raw edges →   ← Align raw edges

Step 4 With <u>right sides together</u>, sew the pillow sham top and back together at top/bottom edges only; press. Turn pillow sham right side out. Insert prepared inner pillow into pillow sham.

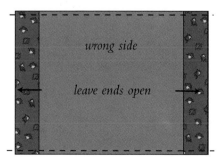

wrong side

leave ends open

Yo-Yo Heart

16-inches square without ruffle

Fabrics & Supplies

18-inch square	**BEIGE PRINT** for pillow top
(25) 4-1/2-inch squares	**ASSORTED PRINTS** for yo-yos
3/8 yard	**ROSE FLORAL** for inner ruffle
3/8 yard	**GREEN PRINT** for outer ruffle
1/2 yard	**ROSE PRINT** for pillow back
18-inch square	**BEIGE** for quilted pillow top lining

18-inch square quilt batting
for quilted pillow top

16-inch pillow form

water erasable marking pen, spray adhesive
for basting

Clover "Quick" Yo-Yo Maker (Large)
or template material for yo-yos

*Before beginning this project,
read through **Getting Started** on page 181.*

Quilt the Pillow Top

Step 1 Use a water erasable marking pen to mark the 18-inch **BEIGE PRINT** pillow top square with a 1-inch wide crosshatch grid.

Basting Suggestions: *We suggest using spray adhesive for basting (follow manufacturer's instructions); or, pin or hand baste the layers together.*

Step 2 Layer the 18-inch **BEIGE** lining square, batting square, and **BEIGE PRINT** pillow top (right side up). Referring to ***Basting Suggestions***, baste the layers together and quilt.

Step 3 Trim quilted pillow top to 16-1/2-inches square. Hand baste raw edges together to prevent them from rippling when ruffle is attached.

Make the Yo-Yos

Our Yo-Yo Heart Pillow was made using the Clover "Quick" Yo-Yo Maker (Large). Follow manufacturer's instructions to make a total of (25) yo-yos which are 1-3/4-inches in diameter.

The following instructions are for making yo-yos without the Clover Yo-Yo Maker.

Step 1 Trace yo-yo pattern on page 149 onto template material; cut out.

Step 2 Using the 4-inch circle template, trace 25 circles on the wrong side of the designated fabrics.

Step 3 To make each yo-yo, turn edges of circle under a scant 1/8-inch. Take care to keep seam allowances of each circle the same size. Use one strand of quilting thread to make running stitches close to the fold. Make stitches approximately 1/4-inch long and 1/4-inch apart. If the running stitches are made too close together, it will be difficult to pull up the stitches to make a nice tight hole at the yo-yo center.

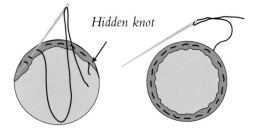

Hidden knot

Step 4 To form yo-yo, pull up gathering thread so the circle is gathered on the right side. Pull thread tight; knot and bury the thread in the fold of the yo-yo. The back side of the yo-yo will be flat. <u>At this point the finished yo-yo should measure 1-3/4-inches in diameter.</u>

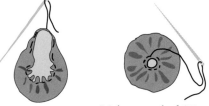

Make a total of 25 yo-yos

Step 5 Referring to Step 6 diagram, position yo-yos on 16-1/2-inch quilted pillow top to make a heart shape. Sew the yo-yos together in rows. To sew the yo-yos together, place them right sides together, stitch them together along their edges with several whipstitches. Make a secure knot; bury the thread and clip it. Sew the rows together in the same manner to make the heart shape.

Step 6 Center the yo-yo heart shape on the 16-1/2-inch quilted pillow top; pin in place. Invisibly tack the yo-yos to pillow top. We suggest tacking the yo-yo centers first, then tack one point on each yo-yo outside edge.

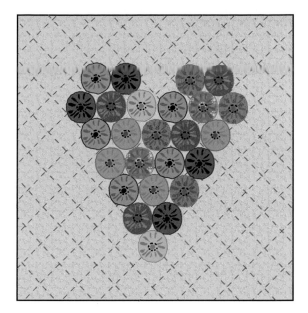

Pillow Ruffle

Note: By sewing 2 different width fabrics together, you form the illusion of a double ruffle without all the additional bulk.

Cutting

From **ROSE PRINT**:

• Cut 4, 2-1/2 x 44-inch inner ruffle strips

From **GREEN PRINT**:

• Cut 4, 3 x 44-inch outer ruffle strips

Piecing and Attaching the Ruffle

Step 1 Diagonally piece together the 2-1/2-inch wide **ROSE** strips.

Step 2 Diagonally piece together the 3-inch wide **GREEN** strips.

Step 3 Aligning long edges, sew together the **ROSE** and **GREEN** strips; press. <u>At this point the ruffle strip should be 5-inches wide.</u>

Step 4 Diagonally piece together the 5-inch wide **ROSE/GREEN** strip to make a continuous ruffle strip. Fold strip in half lengthwise, wrong sides together; press. Divide ruffle strip into 4 equal segments; mark quarter points with safety pins.

Step 5 To gather ruffle, position quilting thread a scant 1/4-inch from raw edges of folded ruffle strip. You will need a length of thread 160-inches long. Secure one end of the thread by stitching across it. Zigzag stitch over the thread all the way around the ruffle strip taking care not to sew through it.

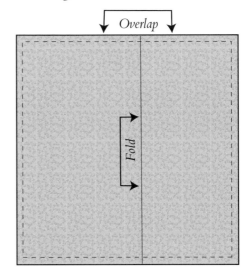

Secure   *zigzag*

Step 6 Divide pillow top edges into 4 equal segments; mark quarter points with safety pins. With right sides together and raw edges aligned, pin ruffle to pillow top, matching quarter points. Gently pull up gathering stitches until ruffle fits pillow top, taking care to allow a little extra fullness in the ruffle at each corner. Sew ruffle to pillow top using a 1/4-inch seam allowance.

Pillow Back

Cutting

From **ROSE PRINT**:

• Cut 2, 16-1/2 x 20-inch rectangles

Assemble the Pillow Back

Step 1 With wrong sides together, fold each 16-1/2 x 20-inch **ROSE** rectangle in half crosswise to make 2, 10 x 16-1/2-inch double thick pillow back pieces. Overlap the 2 folded

edges so the pillow back measures 16-1/2-inches square; pin. Using a scant 1/4-inch seam allowance, stitch around entire pillow piece to create a single pillow back. The double thickness of each pillow back piece will make the pillow more stable and give it a nice finishing touch.

Overlap

Fold

Step 2 With right sides together, layer pillow back and pillow top; pin. The ruffle will be sandwiched between the 2 layers and turned toward pillow center at this time. Pin and stitch around outside edges using a 3/8-inch seam allowance.

Step 3 Turn pillow right side out, insert pillow form through back opening, and fluff up ruffle.

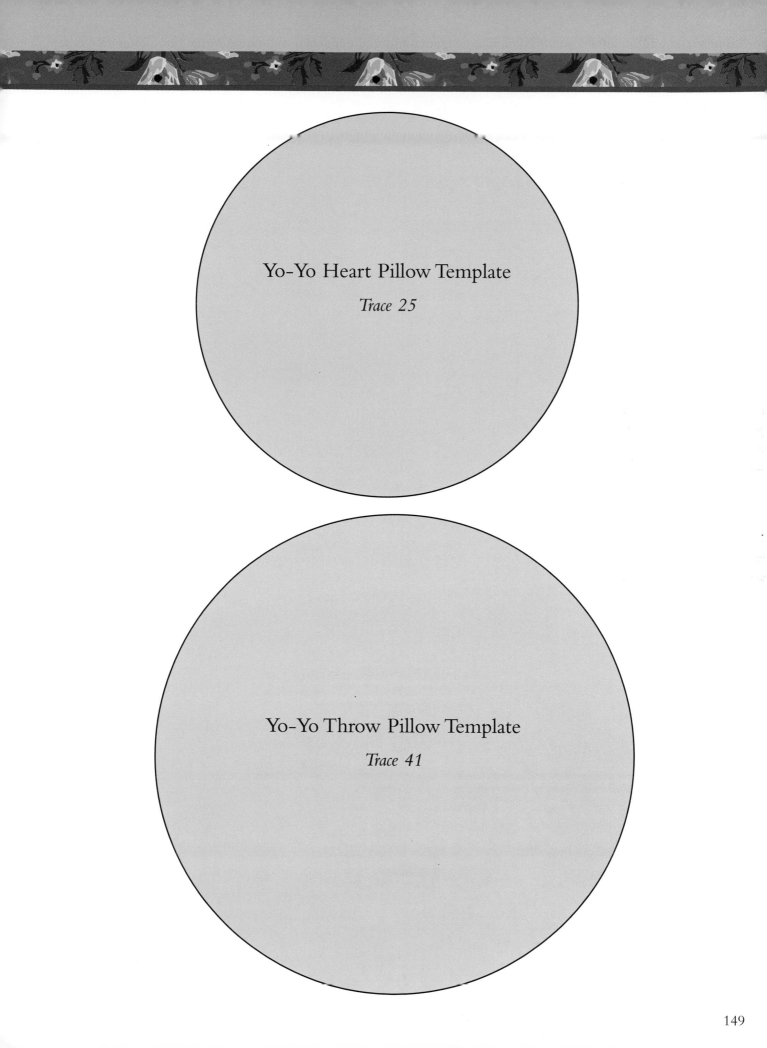

Yo-Yo Heart Pillow Template

Trace 25

Yo-Yo Throw Pillow Template

Trace 41

Yo-Yo Throw

18-inches square

Fabrics & Supplies

1-1/4 yards **GREEN PRINT**
for pillow top, pillow back

(41) 5-1/2-inch squares
ASSORTED PRINTS
for yo-yos

24-inch square **BEIGE** for quilted pillow
top lining

24-inch square quilt batting for quilted pillow top

18-inch pillow form

water erasable marking pen

spray adhesive for basting

Clover "Quick" Yo-Yo Maker (Extra-Large) or
template material for yo-yos

*Before beginning this project,
read through* **Getting Started** *on page 181.*

Pillow Top

Cutting

From **GREEN PRINT**:

• Cut 2, 19 x 24-inch rectangles for pillow back.
Set the rectangles aside.

• Cut 1, 20-inch square for pillow top

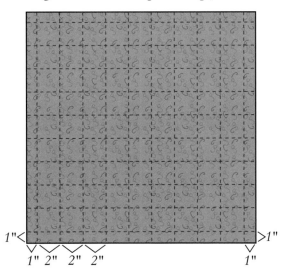

Pillow Top Assembly

Step 1 Referring to the diagram for measurements, use a water erasable marking pen to mark the 20-inch **GREEN** pillow top square for quilting. (Mark 1-inch in from the raw edges. Mark a 2-inch grid through the rest of the pillow top.)

1"< >1"

1" 2" 2" 2" 1"

Basting Suggestions: *We suggest using spray adhesive for basting (follow manufacturer's instructions). If you like, pin or hand baste the layers together before quilting.*

Step 2 Layer the 24-inch **BEIGE** lining square, batting square, and **GREEN** pillow top (right side up). Referring to ***Basting Suggestions***, baste the layers together and quilt.

Step 3 Trim quilted pillow top to 20-inches square. Hand baste raw edges together to prevent them from rippling.

Make the Yo-Yos

Our Yo-Yo Throw Pillow was made using the Clover "Quick" Yo-Yo Maker (Extra-Large). Follow manufacturer's instructions to make a total of (41) yo-yos which are 2-1/4-inches in diameter.

The following instructions are for making yo-yos without the Clover Yo-Yo Maker.

Step 1 Trace yo-yo pattern on page 149 onto template material; cut out.

Step 2 Using the 4-3/4-inch circle template, trace 41 circles on the wrong side of the 5-1/2-inch designated squares.

Step 3 To make each yo-yo, turn edges of circle under a scant 1/8-inch. Take care to keep seam allowances of each circle the same size. Use one strand of quilting thread to make running stitches close to the fold. Make stitches approximately 1/4-inch long and 1/4-inch apart. If the running stitches are made too close together, it will be difficult to pull up the stitches to make a nice tight hole at the yo-yo center.

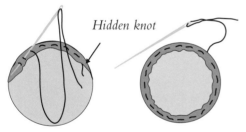
Hidden knot

Step 4 To form yo-yo, pull up gathering thread so the circle is gathered on the right side. Pull thread tight; knot and bury the thread in the fold of the yo-yo. The back side of the yo-yo will be flat. <u>At this point the finished yo-yo should measure 2-1/4-inches in diameter.</u>

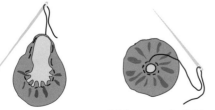
Make a total of 41 yo-yos

Step 5 Referring to the diagram, position the yo-yos on the quilted pillow top. Invisibly tack the yo-yo centers to pillow top.

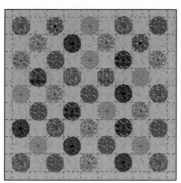

Pillow Back

Cutting

The 2, 19 x 24-inch **GREEN PRINT** backing rectangles were previously cut.

Assemble the Pillow Back

Step 1 With wrong sides together, fold each 19 x 24-inch **GREEN** rectangle in half crosswise to make 2, 12 x 19-inch double thick pillow back pieces. Overlap the 2 folded edges so the pillow back measures 19-inches square; pin. Using a 1/4-inch seam allowance, stitch around entire pillow piece to create a single pillow back. The double thickness of each pillow back piece will make the pillow more stable and give it a nice finishing touch.

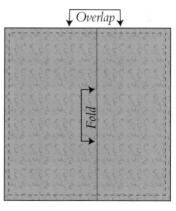
Overlap
Fold

Step 2 Before the pillow top and pillow back are sewn together, you will need to pin the outer yo-yo edges in toward the center of the pillow top so the yo-yo edges won't get caught in the seam allowance. With right sides together, layer pillow back and pillow top; pin. Stitch around outside edges using a 1-inch seam allowance.

Step 3 Turn pillow right side out and remove the pins that are holding the yo-yo edges in place. Insert pillow form through back opening.

Mad for Plaid

18-inches square

Fabrics & Supplies

1/8 yard **GREEN PRINT** for pillow top

1/8 yard **TAN PRINT** for pillow top

1 yard **BROWN FLORAL** for pillow top, border, pillow backing

1/8 yard **BEIGE PRINT** for pillow top

1/8 yard **ROSE PRINT** for pillow top

24-inch square **BEIGE PRINT** for pillow top lining

quilt batting, at least 24-inches square

18-inch pillow form

Sulky® Flying Colors Thread for decorative stitches: (733-1131 Cloister Brown and 733-1180 Medium Taupe)

*Before beginning this project, read through **Getting Started** on page 181.*

Pillow Top

Cutting

From **GREEN PRINT:**
• Cut 2, 2 x 44-inch strips. From strips cut:
  4, 2 x 22-inch strips

From **TAN PRINT**:
• Cut 1, 1-1/2 x 44-inch strip. From strip cut:
  2, 1-1/2 x 22-inch strips

From **BROWN FLORAL**:
• Cut 1, 7 x 44-inch strip. From strip cut:
  1, 7-inch center square
  2, 2-1/2 x 19-inch side border strips
  2, 2-1/2 x 15-inch top/bottom border strips

From **BEIGE PRINT**:
• Cut 1, 2-1/2 x 44-inch strip. From strip cut:
  4, 2-1/2 x 4-1/2-inch rectangles
  4, 2-1/2-inch squares

From **ROSE PRINT**:
• Cut 1, 2-1/2 x 44-inch strip. From strip cut:
  4, 2-1/2-inch squares

Piecing

Refer to arrows on diagraoms for pressing.

Step 1 Aligning long edges, sew together 3 of the 2 x 22-inch **GREEN** strips and the 2, 1-1/2 x 22-inch **TAN** strips. Press seam allowances toward darker strips. Refer to **Hints and Helps for Pressing Strip Sets** on page 187. Cut strip set into segments.

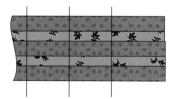

Cut 4, 4-1/2-inch wide segments

Step 2 Sew 2 of the Step 1 segments to the side edges of the 7-inch **BROWN FLORAL** center square. <u>At this point the unit should measure 7 x 15-inches.</u>

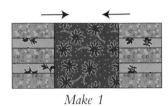

Make 1

Step 3 Sew together the 2-1/2-inch **BEIGE** and **ROSE** squares; press. Make 4 units. Sew the 2-1/2 x 4-1/2-inch **BEIGE** rectangles to the side edge of each of the units; press. <u>At this point each corner square should measure 4-1/2-inches square.</u>

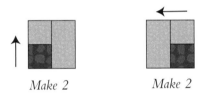

Make 2   *Make 2*

Step 4 Sew the corner squares to both side edges of the remaining Step 1 segments. <u>At this point each unit should measure 4-1/2 x 15-inches.</u>

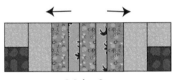

Make 2

Step 5 Sew together the Step 2 and Step 4 units; press. <u>At this point the pillow center should measure 15-inches square.</u>

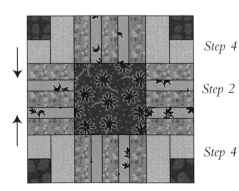

Step 4

Step 2

Step 4

Step 6 Sew the 2-1/2 x 15-inch **BROWN FLORAL** border strips to the top/bottom edges of the pillow center; press. Sew the 2-1/2 x 19-inch **BROWN FLORAL** border strips to the side edges; press.

Quilting the Pillow Top

Step 1 Layer the 24-inch **BEIGE** lining square, batting square, and pieced pillow top (right side up).

Machine Feather Stitch   *Hand Feather Stitch*

Step 2 Pin or hand baste layers together. Our pillow top was machine quilted using a decorative feather stitch. We used Sulky® Flying Colors thread (733-1131 Cloister Brown & 733-1180 Medium Taupe).

taupe

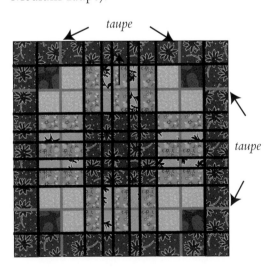

taupe

Step 3 Trim pillow top assembly to 18-1/2-inches square. Hand baste the edges together to prevent them from rippling when the quilted pillow top is sewn to pillow back.

Pillow Back

Cutting

From **BROWN FLORAL**:

• Cut 1, 26 x 44-inch strip. From strip cut: 2, 18-1/2 x 26-inch rectangles for pillow back

Assembly

Step 1 With wrong sides together, fold pillow back rectangles in half crosswise to make 2, 13 x 18-1/2-inch double-thick pillow back pieces. Overlap the 2 folded edges so pillow back measures 18-1/2-inches square. Pin the pieces together and machine baste around entire piece using a 1/4-inch seam allowance to create a single pillow back.

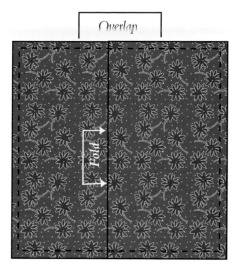

Step 2 With right sides together, layer pillow back and quilted pillow top; pin. Stitch around outside edges. Turn pillow right side out, insert pillow form through back opening.

Mad for Plaid Pillow
18-inches square

Gift Pillow

12 x 16-inches

Fabrics & Supplies

3/8 yard	**BLUE FLORAL** for pillow cover
1/4 yard	**YELLOW DIAGONAL PRINT** for ruffles
5/8 yard	**BLUE PRINT** for envelope, facings
3/8 yard	**YELLOW DOT** for envelope flap, inner pillow

12 x 16-inch pillow form

(2) 13 x 18-inch rectangles of quilt batting

temporary basting spray

1-inch decorative button

*Before beginning this project,
read through **Getting Started** on page 181.*

Inner Pillow

Cutting

From **YELLOW DOT**:

• Cut 2, 12-1/2 x 16-1/2-inch rectangles

Piecing Inner Pillow Cover

Step 1 With right sides facing, sew together the 12-1/2 x 16-1/2-inch **YELLOW DOT** rectangles leaving a 9-inch opening on one side for turning.

Step 2 Turn pillow case right side out, insert pillow form; sew opening closed.

Pillow Cover

Cutting

From **BLUE FLORAL**:

• Cut 1, 13 x 44-inch strip. From strip cut:
  2, 13 x 18-inch rectangles for pillow cover

From **BLUE PRINT**:

• Cut 1, 13 x 44-inch strip. From strip cut:
  2, 13 x 18-inch rectangles for pillow lining
  1, 6-1/2 x 8-1/2-inch rectangle for pocket
• Cut 2, 2 x 26-inch strips for facings

From **YELLOW DOT**:

• Cut 1, 6-1/2 x 8-1/2-inch rectangle
  for pocket lining/flap

Assembly

Step 1 First layer: 13 x 18-inch **BLUE PRINT** pillow lining (wrong side up), lightly spray with basting adhesive. Second layer: batting, lightly spray with basting adhesive. Third layer: **BLUE FLORAL** pillow cover (right side up). Pat all layers in place. Machine quilt the pillow cover unit with a meander design. Repeat this step using the remaining rectangles. <u>Trim each unit to 12-1/2 x 16-1/2-inches.</u>

Step 2 To make the decorative pocket, <u>layer</u> the 6-1/2 x 8-1/2-inch **BLUE PRINT** and **YELLOW DOT** rectangles with right sides together. Draw diagonal lines for the flap angles referring to the diagram. Stitch on the lines and trim the seam allowances to 1/4-inch. Sew the remaining edges together using a 1/4-inch seam allowance leaving a 4-inch opening along the bottom edge for turning. Turn the pocket right side out; press. Hand sew the opening closed.

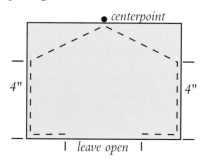

● *centerpoint*

4"   4"

| *leave open* |

Step 3 Turn the flap down; pin in place. Center the prepared pocket on one of the quilted pillow cover rectangles. Edge stitch the pocket in place leaving the top edge open for inserting "gift."

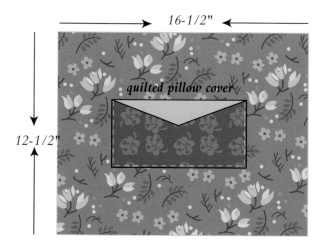

16-1/2"

quilted pillow cover

12-1/2"

Step 4 With right sides together, sew the 2 quilted pillow covers together along the top/bottom 16-1/2-inch edges; turn right side out.

Ruffles and Facings

Cutting

From **YELLOW DIAGONAL PRINT**:

• Cut 3, 2-1/2 x 44-inch strips. Diagonally piece strips together to make 1 strip. Cut the strip in half to make 2, 2-1/2 x 63-inch ruffle strips.

From **BLUE PRINT**:

• Cut 2, 2 x 26-inch facing strips

Attach Ruffle

Step 1 Diagonally piece the ends of each ruffle strip together to make 2 continuous ruffle strips. Fold each strip in half lengthwise, wrong sides together; press. Divide ruffle strips into 4 equal segments; mark quarter points with safety pins.

Step 2 To gather each ruffle, position a 63-inch length of heavyweight thread a scant 1/4-inch in from the raw edge of the folded ruffle strip. Secure the end of the thread by stitching across it. Zigzag stitch over the thread all the way around the ruffle strip taking care not to sew through the thread.

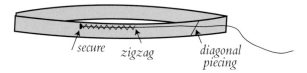

secure   *zigzag*   *diagonal piecing*

Step 3 With right sides together and raw edges aligned, pin ruffle to the side edges of the quilted pillow cover matching quarter points; pin in place. Gently pull gathering stitches until ruffle fits pillow cover; pin and machine baste using a 1/4-inch seam allowance.

Step 4 To make a facing, with right sides together, fold a 2 x 26-inch **BLUE PRINT** strip in half lengthwise; press. Fold one facing end under 1/2-inch. With right sides together and raw edges aligned, sew the facing to the pillow cover overlapping the ends. The ruffle will be sandwiched between the facing and the pillow cover.

Step 5 Bring the facing to the inside of the pillow cover and hand stitch in place. At this point the ruffle should be standing straight out. Repeat to attach the facing to the other side.

Step 6 Attach button to pocket to hold flap in place. Insert inner pillow into pillow cover.

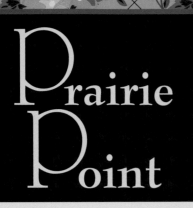

Prairie Point

18 x 25-inches

Fabrics & Supplies

1/4 yard **BLUE PRINT**
for pillow top (upper section)

1-3/8 yards **LARGE BLUE FLORAL**
for pillow top (lower section,
covered buttons, and pillow back)

1/3 yard **RUST PRINT** for prairie points

(5) 1-1/8-inch diameter buttons

18 x 25-inch bed pillow

*Before beginning this project,
read through **Getting Started** on page 181.*

Pillow Top and Prairie Points

Cutting

From **BLUE PRINT**:
- Cut 1, 7-1/2 x 25-1/2-inch rectangle
  for upper section

From **LARGE BLUE FLORAL**:
- Cut 1, 11-1/2 x 25-1/2-inch rectangle
  for lower section

From **RUST PRINT**:
- Cut 2, 4-1/2 x 44-inch strips. From strips cut:
  11, 4-1/2-inch squares

Prepare Prairie Points and Assemble Pillow Top

Step 1 To make prairie points, fold a 4-1/2-inch **RUST**
square in half diagonally, wrong sides together; press.
Fold the triangle in half again; press.

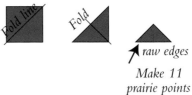

*Make 11
prairie points*

Step 2 With raw edges aligned, pin the prairie points
to the long top edge of the **LARGE BLUE
FLORAL** rectangle. Overlap prairie points slightly,
adjusting them to fit the top edge;
baste in place.

Step 3 With right sides together, layer the **BLUE PRINT** rectangle on the top edge of the **LARGE BLUE FLORAL** rectangle. The prairie points will be sandwiched between the 2 layers. Sew the layers together; press.

Prairie points are sandwiched between the layers

Step 4 Sew the buttons to the pillow top.

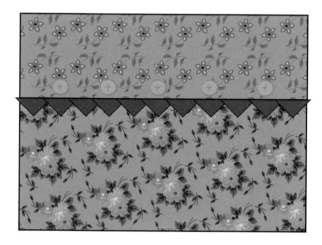

Pillow Back

Cutting

From **LARGE BLUE FLORAL**:
• Cut 2, 18-1/2 x 35-inch pillow back rectangles

Assembling the Pillow Back

Step 1 With wrong sides together, fold each **LARGE BLUE FLORAL** pillow back rectangle in half crosswise to make 2, 17-1/2 x 18-1/2-inch double-thick pillow back pieces. Overlap the 2 folded edges so the pillow back measures 18-1/2 x 25-1/2-inches. Pin the pieces together and machine baste around the entire piece to create a single pillow back, using a

scant 1/4-inch seam allowance. The double thickness of the pillow back will make it more stable and give it a nice finishing touch.

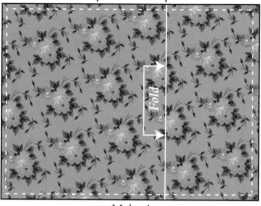

Overlap

Fold

Make 1

Step 2 With right sides together, layer pillow back and pillow top; pin. Stitch around the outside edges using a 1/4-inch seam allowance. Turn pillow right side out and insert pillow through back opening.

small gifts

Strip Pieced Bag

13-1/2 x 16-inches

Fabrics & Supplies

6 x 44-inch strips of **6 ASSORTED PRINTS** for bag

1/2 yard **FLORAL** for lining

1/2 yard **COORDINATING PRINT** for binding, straps

18 x 36-inch rectangle batting for foundation piecing

1/4-inch wide cotton cording for straps, (2)10-inches long

Before beginning this project, read through **Getting Started** *on page 181.*

Bag Assembly

Cutting

From *each* of the **6 ASSORTED PRINTS**:
- Cut 3, 2-1/2 x 20-inch strips

From batting:
- Cut 1, 18 x 36-inch rectangle

From **FLORAL**:
- Cut 1, 16 x 35-inch rectangle for lining

Assembly

Step 1 Draw vertical lines on the batting as a guide to help keep the strips straight while they are stitched in place.

guide lines

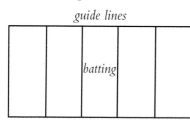

Step 2 Position a 2-1/2-inch wide **ASSORTED PRINT** strip, right side up, on the left edge of batting. Now position a second 2-1/2-inch wide strip, wrong side up, on top of the first strip. Stitch through the 3

thicknesses, 1/4-inch from the right aligned raw edges. Fold back the second strip and finger-press or lightly iron.

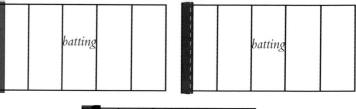

Step 3 Continue adding the strips in this manner until the batting is completely covered. Be very careful to keep the strips parallel to the edges of the batting.

Step 4 Trim the strip pieced unit to 16 x 35-inches. With rights sides together, fold the prepared strip pieced rectangle in half crosswise. Stitch the side/bottom seams of the bag using a 1/4-inch seam allowance; press.

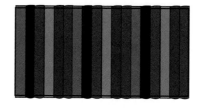

16"

fold

17-1/2"

Step 5 Fold the bottom flat. Stitch across both triangle tips approximately 1-3/4-inches in from each point and hand-tack the triangle tips down to the bottom seam line. Turn tote right side out.

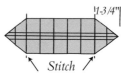

1-3/4"

Stitch

Step 6 With right sides together, fold the **FLORAL** lining rectangle in half crosswise. Stitch the side/bottom seams of the lining using a 1/4-inch seam allowance; press. Make a flat bottom for the lining as in Step 5. With wrong sides together, insert the lining into the bag. Pin or baste the top raw edges together.

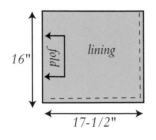

Step 3 With raw edges aligned, position the straps evenly on the outside of the bag (about 4-1/2-inches from the sides). Stitch in place.

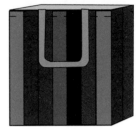

Strap Assembly

Cutting

From **COORDINATING PRINT**:
- Cut 2, 5 x 30-inch strips (or to desired length).

From cording:
- Cut 2, 10-inch long pieces

Assembly

Step 1 To make the straps, with wrong sides together, fold both long edges of the 5 x 30-inch **COORDINATING PRINT** strips to meet in the center; press. Fold in half again so the strips measure 1-1/4 x 30-inches; press. Topstitch the edges.

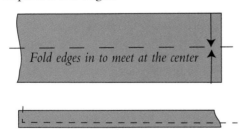

Step 2 Position the 10-inch long cording on the center of the strap. Wrap the strap over the cording and stitch the folded edges together. Stitch the strap at each end of the cording to keep it in place.

Binding

Cutting

From **COORDINATING PRINT**:
- Cut 1, 6-1/2 x 44-inch strip for binding

Attaching the Binding

Step 1 Fold the strip in half lengthwise, wrong sides together; press. Trim one end at a 45° angle; turn end under 3/8-inch; press. With <u>right sides together</u> and raw edges aligned, stitch the binding to the top raw edge of the bag using a 1-inch seam allowance. The straps will be layered between the bag and binding.

Step 2 Turn the folded edge of the binding over the top raw edge and to the inside of the bag. Hand stitch the binding in place.

Step 3 Flip the straps up and machine stitch them in place to secure them to the binding.

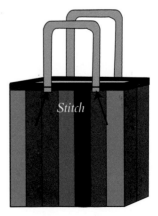

Simple Notebook Cover

Designed for a 9-3/4 x 7-inch composition notebook

Fabrics & Supplies

1/3 yard   **PRINT** for cover

9-3/4 x 7-1/2-inch Marble Composition notebook

*Before beginning this project,
read through **Getting Started** on page 181.*

Cutting

From **PRINT**:
• Cut 1, 12 x 24-inch rectangle

Assembly

Step 1   On 12-inch sides, make double 1/4-inch hems; press and stitch.

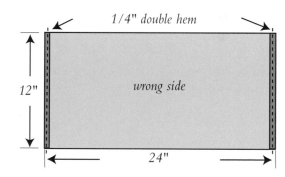

1/4" double hem

12"

wrong side

24"

Step 2   With right side facing up, fold back both 12-inch sides 3-5/8-inches; pin. (Adjust the folded measurement to fit your notebook.) Stitch along the upper and lower edges 1-inch from the raw edges on each side.

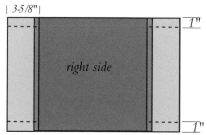

3-5/8"

1"

right side

1"

Step 3   Turn ends right side out and insert your notebook.

Blossom Needle Case

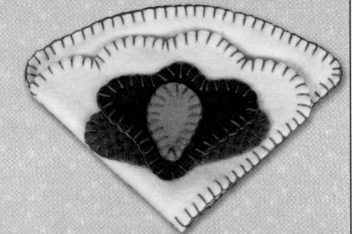

7-1/2 x 5-1/2-inches

Fabrics & Supplies

(2) 7 x 11-inch rectangles **WHITE WOOL** for
needle case inside & outside

4-1/2-inch square   **ROSE WOOL** for flower

2-1/2-inch square   **GOLD WOOL** for flower center

4-inch square   **GREEN WOOL** for leaves

pearl cotton for decorative stitches: gold

3/8-inch snap for closure

*Before beginning this project,
read through **Getting Started** on page 181.*

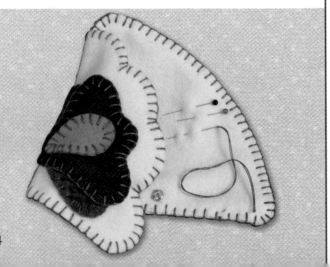

Appliqué the Needle Case

Step 1   To make templates, trace the shapes on pages 164 and 165, onto paper and cut out. Trace all the shapes onto the designated **WOOL** and cut out on the drawn line.

Step 2   Referring to the placement diagram on page 165, position the flower/leaf applique shapes on the outside layer of the **WHITE WOOL** needle case. Blanket stitch the leaves in place first, then the flower, and lastly the flower center.

Note: To prevent hand blanket stitches from "rolling off" the edges of the applique shapes, take an extra backstitch in the same place as you made the blanket stitch, going around outer curves, corners, and points. For straight edges, taking a backstitch every inch is enough.

Step 3   With wrong sides together, layer the two **WHITE WOOL** shapes; pin. Stitch a running stitch along the fold line going through both layers. Blanket stitch the edges together.

Step 4   Position the snap pieces on the inside of the needle case and carefully hand stitch in place. These stitches should not show on the outside of the case.

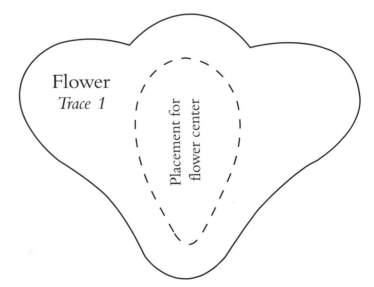

Flower
Trace 1

Placement for flower center

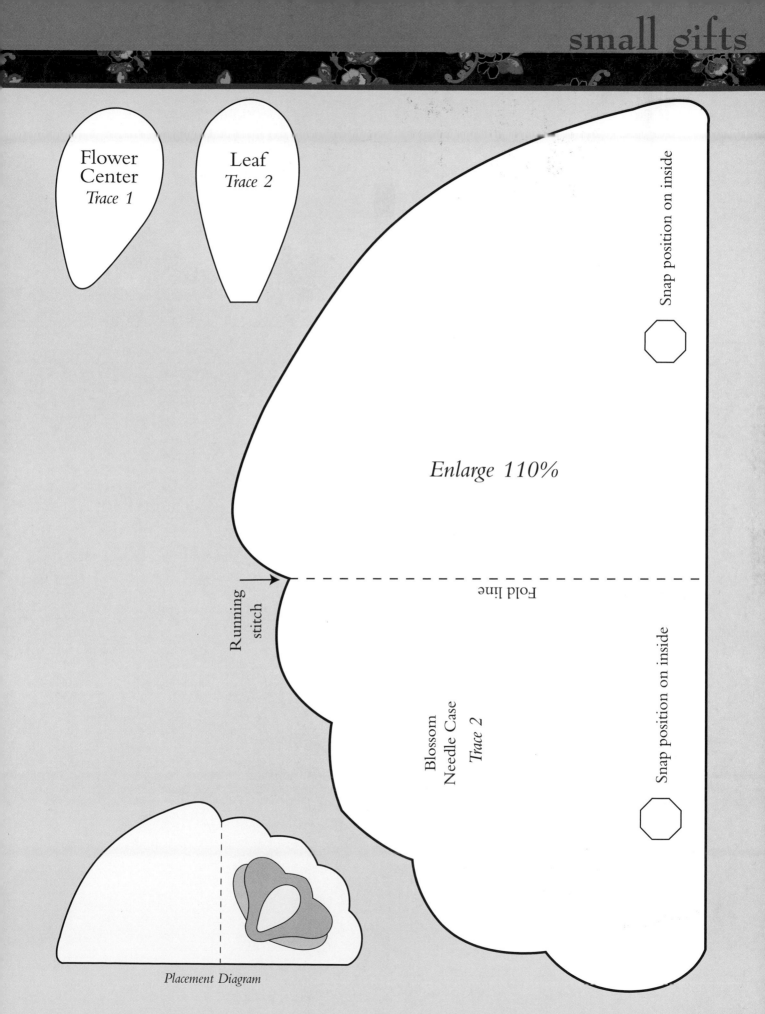

Flower
Center
Trace 1

Leaf
Trace 2

Snap position on inside

Enlarge 110%

Running
stitch

Fold line

Snap position on inside

Blossom
Needle Case
Trace 2

Placement Diagram

Pocket Tote

14-inches high x 14-inches wide

Fabrics & Supplies

3/4 yard	**BLACK/GOLD FLORAL** for tote
1-1/4 yards	**GOLD PRINT** for lining, bottom support, binding
10-inch square	**GREEN PRINT** for pocket
1/3 yard	**BROWN PRINT** for handles, pocket lining

muslin lining for quilting tote cover (27 x 40-inches)

quilt batting for quilting tote cover (27 x 40-inches)

heavy weight interfacing to strengthen handles (10 x 30-inches)

cardboard for tote bottom stabilizer (9 x 14-inches)

decorative button (7/8-inch diameter)

*Before beginning this project, read through **Getting Started** on page 181.*

Quilting the Tote Cover

Cutting

From **BLACK/GOLD FLORAL**:

• Cut 1, 27 x 40-inch rectangle

Step 1 On flat surface, layer the 27 x 40-inch rectangles of muslin lining, quilt batting, and **BLACK/GOLD FLORAL** right side facing up. Quilt as desired. Our project was quilted in a meandering pattern.

Step 2 Trim quilted tote cover to 25 x 38-inches. Hand baste 1/4-inch away from outer edges to secure.

Pocket and Tote Assembly

Cutting

From **GREEN PRINT**:

• Cut 1, 8-1/2-inch square for pocket

From **BROWN PRINT**:

• Cut 1, 8-1/2-inch square for pocket lining
• Cut 2, 5 x 30-inch strips for handles
    (or to desired length) – set aside

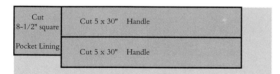

Cutting diagram for brown print

Assembly

Step 1 To make the pocket, with right sides together, layer the 8-1/2-inch **GREEN** and **BROWN** squares. Sew the squares together leaving 3-inches open on one side for turning. Turn unit right side out. Slip stitch opening closed.

Step 2 Referring to diagram, position pocket on right side of quilted tote cover (2-inches from top edge). Stitch 2 lower side edges of pocket in place. <u>Do not stitch upper side edges.</u> Stitch upper edge in place (about 1-3/4-inch down from pocket tip). At this point there will be a

5-inch opening on the 2 upper side edges of the pocket. Fold the pocket tip over to cover stitching. Secure with decorative button.

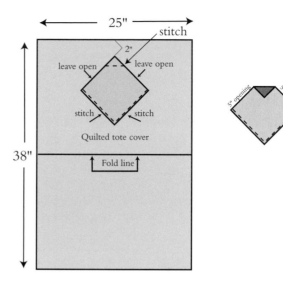

Step 3 With right sides together, fold tote in half crosswise so it measures 25-inches across the top and 19-inches high. Stitch the 19-inch sides together with a 1/2-inch seam allowance.

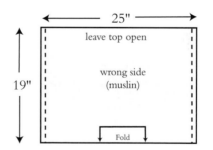

Step 4 To make a flat bottom, with the tote inside out, fold bottom so a 4-1/2-inch triangle is formed at each end. Stitch on fold lines and press triangle tips down to the bottom. Turn tote right side out.

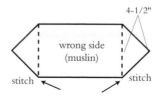

Lining and Binding

Cutting

From **GOLD PRINT**:

- Cut 1, 25 x 38-inch rectangle
- Cut 2, 4 x 44-inch binding strips.
      Diagonally piece strips together.

Assembly

Step 1 With right sides together, fold the 25 x 38-inch **GOLD** rectangle in half crosswise so it measures 25-inches across the top and 19-inches high as in Step 3, Pocket and Tote Assembly. Stitch the 19-inch sides together with a 1/2-inch seam allowance.

Step 2 To make a flat bottom, with lining inside out, fold the bottom so a 4-1/2-inch triangle is formed at each end. Stitch on the fold lines and press the triangle tips down to the bottom as you did for the tote in Step 4, Pocket and Tote Assembly. Leave lining inside out.

Step 3 With wrong sides facing, slip lining unit inside the quilted tote. Pin and machine baste top edges together. Tote should be right side out at this time.

Step 4 Bind top edge of tote with the 4-inch wide **GOLD** binding strip. Prepare binding referring to **Binding** on page 189 for complete instructions. Sew binding to top edge of tote using a 1/2-inch seam allowance.

Handles

Cutting

BROWN PRINT – The (2) 5 x 30-inch handle strips were previously cut.

From interfacing:

- Cut 2, 4-7/8 x 30-inch strips (or to desired length)

Assembly

Step 1 Position an interfacing strip on the wrong side of each **BROWN** handle strip. Turn in each narrow end 1/2-inch; press. Fold both long edges in to meet at center; press. Fold

strip in half again; topstitch the 4 edges. At this point each handle should measure 1-1/4-inches wide.

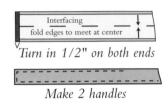

Turn in 1/2" on both ends

Make 2 handles

Step 2 Position each handle on the outside of the tote (7-inches from each side seam); pin in place. Stitch handle in place with a big X.

Bottom Stabilizer

Cutting

From **GOLD PRINT**:

- Cut 1, 9-1/2 x 30-inch rectangle

From cardboard:

- Cut 1, 9 x 14-inch rectangle

Assembly

Step 1 Fold the 9-1/2 x 30-inch **GOLD** rectangle in half crosswise, right sides together. Stitch side seams together with a 1/4-inch seam allowance. Turn right side out.

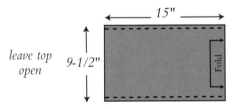

Step 2 Insert cardboard rectangle into the **GOLD** covering. Tuck raw edges inside the covering; stitch opening closed.

Step 3 Position covered cardboard into bottom of tote to stabilize it.

Drawstring Quilt Bag

20 x 33-inches

Fabrics & Supplies

1-1/4 yards   **PRINT** for quilt bag

1-1/2 yards twill tape for tie

seam ripper and safety pin

*Before beginning this project,
read through **Getting Started** on page 181.*

Assembling the Quilt Bag

Cutting

From **PRINT**:

• Cut 1, 40-inch square for quilt bag

Step 1 Referring to the Step 2 diagram, with right sides together, fold the square in half and sew the bottom and side raw edges together using a 3/8-inch seam allowance; press.

Step 2 Turn the open edge under 1/2-inch; press. Turn the same edge under 6-inches; press. Topstitch the folded edge in place to make a large casing.

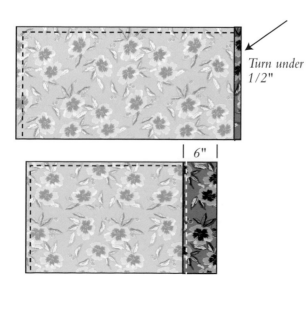

Turn under 1/2"

6"

Step 3 Using a seam ripper, carefully remove a few stitches (about 1-inch in length) from the inside side seam. This opening is for inserting the twill tape. Hand tack the edges of the opening to secure them. Pin the safety pin to the end of the twill tape and insert it into the small opening. Thread the twill tape through the large casing. Turn the bag right side out; press.

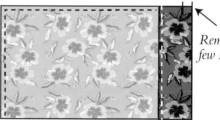

Remove a few stitches

Step 4 Roll up your quilt so it will fit into the quilt bag. Insert the quilt into the quilt bag and pull the drawstring tight; tie.

Note: *This bag can be used as a pillowcase omitting the drawstring.*

Planner Cover

Designed for a 5 x 7-inch spiral bound notebook

Fabrics & Supplies

1/3 yard **BLACK/GOLD FLORAL** for outer cover, inner pocket, center band

1/3 yard **TAN PRINT** for lining

1/3 yard **BROWN PRINT** for binding accent trim (cut on the bias)

1/3 yard **GOLD PRINT** for loop closure, binding (cut on the bias)

quilt batting, at least 10 x 36-inches

3/4-inch diameter button for closure

5 x 7-inch spiral bound notebook

*Before beginning this project,
read through **Getting Started** on page 181.*

Prepare the Cover

Cutting

From **BLACK/GOLD FLORAL**:

• Cut 1, 10 x 18-inch rectangle for outer cover

From **TAN PRINT**:

• Cut 1, 10 x 18-inch rectangle for lining

From batting:

• Cut 1, 10 x 18-inch rectangle

Piecing

Step 1 With right sides facing out, layer the 10 x 18-inch **BLACK/GOLD FLORAL** and **TAN** rectangles with the batting sandwiched between the layers.

Step 2 Quilt the unit as desired. Our sample was crosshatched. Trim the unit to 8 x 16-1/4-inches.

Step 3 Trim one end of the unit using the curved shape on page 173 for the top flap. Hand baste all 3 layers together a scant 1/4-inch from the edge.

Inner Pocket and Center Band

Cutting

From **BLACK/GOLD FLORAL**:
- Cut 1, 8-inch square for inner pocket
- Cut 2, 4 x 8-inch rectangles for center band

From batting:
- Cut 2, 4 x 8-inch rectangles

Assembly

Step 1 Make the inner pocket: With <u>wrong</u> sides facing, fold the 8-inch **BLACK/GOLD FLORAL** square in half; press. Sandwich a 4 x 8-inch batting rectangle between the 2 layers. Quilt the unit as desired; topstitch the folded edge.

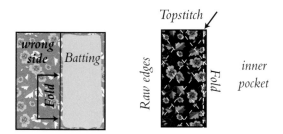

Step 2 With raw edges aligned, position the inner pocket unit along the straight edge of the **TAN** lining side of the unit; baste the raw edges together.

Step 3 To make the center band: With <u>wrong</u> sides of the 4 x 8-inch **BLACK/GOLD FLORAL** rectangles facing, sandwich a 4 x 8-inch batting rectangle between the 2 layers. Quilt the unit as desired. Turn under 1/2-inch on both long edges; topstitch the folded edges.

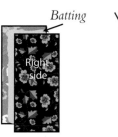

Step 4 With raw edges aligned, position the center band on the **TAN** lining side of the unit; baste the raw edges together.

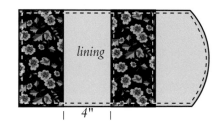

Binding and Accent Trim

Cutting

From **GOLD FLORAL**:
- Cut enough 2-3/4-inch wide **bias** binding strips to make a 50-inch long strip. Diagonally piece the strips together.
- Cut 1, 2 x 4-inch rectangle for loop closure

From **BROWN PRINT**:
- Cut enough 1-inch wide **bias** accent trim strips to make a 40-inch long strip. Diagonally piece the strips together.
- Cut 1, 1 x 8-inch **bias** accent trim strip

Attach Loop Closure and Binding

Step 1 Make the loop closure: Fold both long edges of the 2 x 4-inch **GOLD FLORAL** rectangle in to the center of the rectangle; press. Fold in half again so it is 1/2-inch wide; press and topstitch. Fold the strip in half crosswise to make a loop. Position the loop on the **TAN** lining side of the unit; baste the raw edges together.

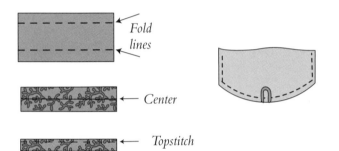

Fold lines

Center

Topstitch

Step 2 With <u>wrong sides</u> together, fold the 1 x 8-inch **BROWN bias** strip in half lengthwise; press. With <u>right sides</u> together and aligning raw edges, position this accent trim strip on the straight edge of the unit. Using a scant 1/4-inch seam allowance, machine baste in place.

Stitch

Right side

Step 3 With <u>wrong sides</u> together, fold the 1 x 40-inch **BROWN bias** strip in half lengthwise; press. With <u>right sides</u> together and aligning raw edges, machine baste this accent trim strip to the side and curved edges of the unit using a scant 1/4-inch seam allowance.

Ease in extra accent trim fabric along the curve so it won't "cup." The ends of the accent trim strips will overlap at the corners. Trim the ends as needed.

Stitch

Right side

Step 4 Prepare the 2-3/4-inch wide *bias* **GOLD FLORAL** binding strips referring to *Binding* on page 189 for complete instructions. Sew the **GOLD FLORAL** binding strips to the unit. Ease in extra binding fabric along the curve so it won't "cup." Approximately 1/8-inch of the **BROWN** accent trim will be visible once the binding is complete. The accent trim is narrow and it will lay flat so you don't need to tack it down.

Step 5 Sew the button approximately 4-inches in from the straight edge for the loop closure. Adjust the button measurement as needed.

Step 6 Insert the front cover of the notebook into the inner pocket and insert the back cover under the center band. Wrap the cover around the notebook and secure the loop closure around the button.

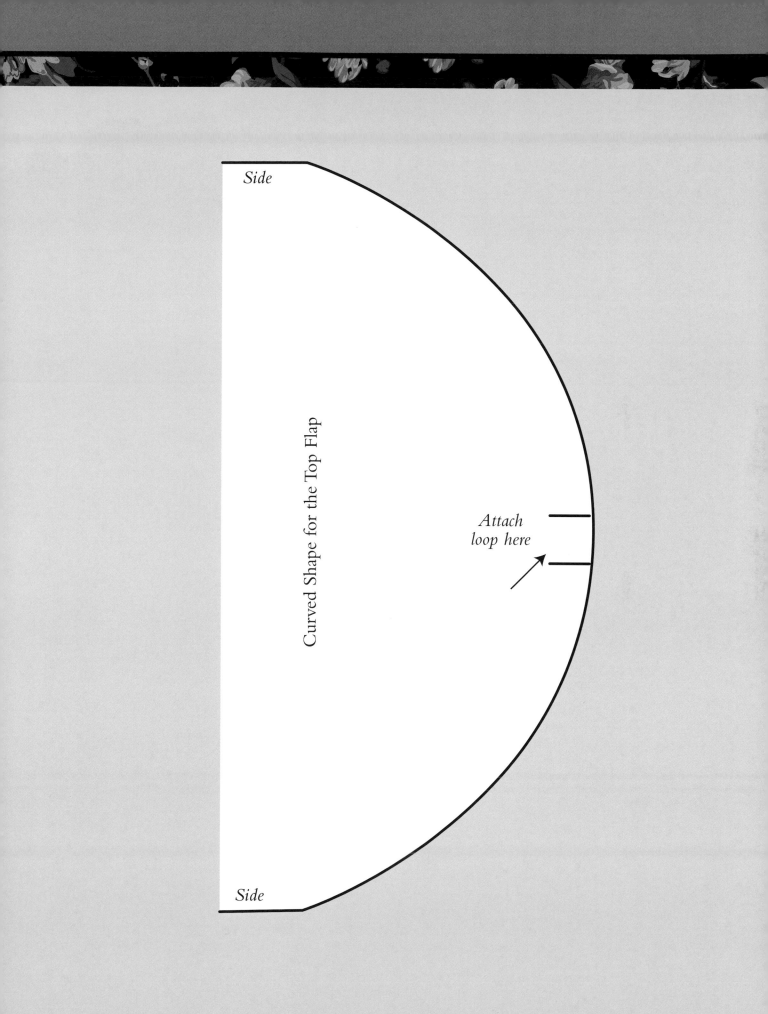

Side

Curved Shape for the Top Flap

Attach
loop here

Side

Strip Pieced Notebook Cover

Designed for a 10 x 11-1/2 x 1-1/2"-inch 3-ring notebook binder

Fabrics & Supplies

3-ring notebook binder (10" x 11-1/2" x 1-1/2" spine width) you will have to alter your measurements if your binder is a different size

1/8 yard   of at least **5 ASSORTED PRINTS** for strip pieced cover

3/8 yard   **DARK PRINT** for inner pocket, center band

1/2 yard   **MEDIUM PRINT** for lining

1/2 yard   **DARK PRINT** for closure, binding

needlepunch batting, at least 15 x 44-inch rectangle for foundation piecing, inner pocket, center band

1-inch diameter button for closure

several plastic sheet protectors to fit your binder

Before beginning this project,
read through **Getting Started** *on page 181.*

Strip Pieced Cover

Cutting

From **ASSORTED PRINTS**:

• Cut a variety of strips to make a 15 x 32-inch rectangle:

       1 x 15-inch strips

       1-1/4 x 15-inch strips

       1-1/2 x 15-inch strips

       1-3/4 x 15-inch strips

       2 x 15-inch strips

From needlepunch batting:

• Cut 1, 15 x 32-inch rectangle.
  This batting rectangle will serve as the foundation for the strip piecing.

Assembly

Step 1 Referring to Diagram 1, position a **PRINT** strip, right side up, on the left short end of the batting foundation rectangle, but do not stitch. Referring to Diagram 2, position a second **PRINT** strip on the first strip, right sides together; aligning raw edges. Stitch through the 3 thicknesses, 1/4-inch from the aligned raw edges. Fold back the second strip and finger-press or lightly iron. Referring to Diagram 3, continue to add strips in varying widths and **PRINTS** until the foundation is completely covered. Be very careful to keep the strips parallel to the edges of the foundation rectangle.

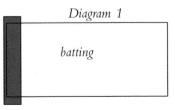

Diagram 1

batting

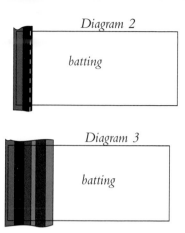

Diagram 2

batting

Diagram 3

batting

Step 2 When the strip piecing is complete, trim the rectangle to 12-1/2-inches x 30-inches (or 1-inch taller than your binder by 8-1/2-inches wider than your binder when it is laying open).

Step 3 With <u>wrong</u> sides together, layer the strip pieced unit on the **MEDIUM PRINT** lining rectangle. Trim the lining even with the strip pieced unit; hand baste the layers together.

Inner Pocket and Center Band

Cutting

From **DARK PRINT**:

• Cut 1, 12-1/2-inch square for inner pocket
• Cut 2, 6 x 12-1/2-inch rectangles for center band

From needlepunch batting:
• Cut 2, 6 x 12-1/2-inch rectangles

Assembly

Step 1 Make the inner pocket: With <u>wrong</u> sides facing, fold the 12-1/2-inch **DARK PRINT** square in half; press. Sandwich a 6 x 12-1/2-inch batting rectangle between the 2 layers. Quilt the unit as desired; topstitch the folded edge.

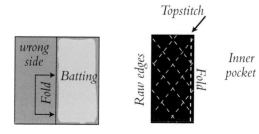

Topstitch

wrong side *Batting* *Fold*

Raw edges *Fold* *Inner pocket*

Step 2 Lay the strip pieced cover out flat with the **MEDIUM PRINT** (lining) facing up. Referring to the diagram below, position the inner pocket on the left edge; baste the raw edges together with a 3/8-inch seam allowance. Make sure your binder fits into this inner pocket.

Step 3 Make the center band: With <u>wrong</u> sides of the 6 x 12-1/2-inch **DARK PRINT** rectangles facing, sandwich a 6 x 12-1/2-inch batting rectangle between the 2 layers. Quilt the unit as desired. Turn under 1/2-inch on both long edges; topstitch the folded edges.

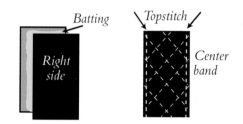

Batting *Topstitch*

Right side *Center band*

Step 4 Referring to the diagram below, position the center band about 14-1/2-inches from the left edge; baste the raw edges together with a 3/8-inch seam allowance. Make sure your binder fits into this center band.

Note: If the spine on the binder is wider than 1-1/2-inches, the center band will need to be positioned a little farther toward the right edge.

Step 5 Trim the right edge using the curved shape on page 177 for the flap. Hand baste the layers together a scant 1/4-inch from the edge.

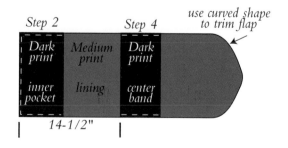

Step 2 *Step 4* *use curved shape to trim flap*

Dark print *Medium print* *Dark print*

inner pocket *lining* *center band*

14-1/2"

Binding and Loop Closure

Note: *The notebook cover will be bound like a quilt with a 3/8-inch seam allowance.*

Cutting

From **DARK PRINT**:

- Cut enough 2-3/4-inch wide **bias** strips to make a 90-inch long strip. Diagonally piece the strips together.

- Cut 1, 2 x 4-inch rectangle for loop closure

Attach the Loop Closure and Binding

Step 1 Make the loop closure: Fold both long edges of the 2 x 4-inch **DARK PRINT** rectangle in to the center of the rectangle; press. Fold in half again so it is 1/2-inch wide; press and topstitch. Fold the strip in half crosswise to make a loop. Position the loop on the <u>lining side</u> of the unit; baste the raw edges together.

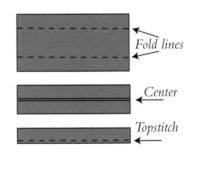

Fold lines

Center

Topstitch

lining

Step 2 Bind the unit referring to **Binding** on page 189 for complete instructions.

Step 3 Insert the binder into the strip pieced notebook cover. Wrap the cover around the binder to locate where to position the button. Sew the button in place; secure the loop closure around the button. As you fill up your binder with pages, you may need to move the button over.

attach the loop here

Curved shape for the flap

Side

Place on fold to make template

Easy Tote

11 x 16-inches

Fabrics & Supplies

1/2 yard **LARGE PRINT** for tote

7/8 yard **COORDINATING PRINT** for lining, binding, handle

Texture Magic™ 47 x 18-inch package

(2) 1-1/8 x 27-inch quilt batting strips for handles

*Before beginning this project, read through **Getting Started** on page 181.*

Tote Assembly

Cutting

From **LARGE PRINT**:

• Cut 1, 18 x 44-inch strip for tote

From **COORDINATING PRINT**:

• Cut 1, 14 x 33-inch rectangle for lining
• Cut 1, 2-3/4 x 42-inch strip for binding
• Cut 2, 5 x 28-inch strips for handles

Assembly

Step 1 Follow **Texture Magic**™ instructions to prepare the **LARGE PRINT** for tote. <u>When the shrinking process is complete, trim the</u> **LARGE PRINT** <u>to 14 x 33-inches.</u>

Step 2 With right sides together, fold the prepared **LARGE PRINT** rectangle in half crosswise. Stitch the side/bottom seams of the tote using a 1/4-inch seam allowance; press.

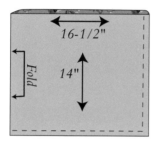

Step 3 Fold the bottom flat. Stitch across both triangle tips approximately 2-1/2-inches in from each point and hand-tack the triangle tips down to the seam line. Turn tote right side out.

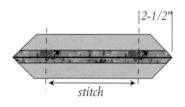

Step 4 With right sides together, fold the **COORDINATING PRINT** lining rectangle in half crosswise. Stitch the side/bottom seams of the lining using a 1/4-inch seam allowance; press. Make a flat bottom for the lining as in Step 3. With wrong sides together, insert the lining into the tote. Pin or baste the top raw edges together.

Step 5 Bind the top raw edges of the tote with the 2-3/4-inch wide **COORDINATING PRINT** binding strip. To do so, fold the strip in half lengthwise, wrong sides together; press. Trim one end at a 45° angle; turn end under 3/8-inch; press. With <u>right sides together</u> and raw edges aligned, stitch the binding to the top raw edge of the tote using a 3/8-inch seam allowance. Trim the end of the binding so it

can be tucked inside the beginning binding about 1/2-inch. Finish stitching the seam. Turn the folded edge of the binding over the top raw edge and to the inside of the tote. Hand stitch the binding in place.

Step 6 To make the handles, with wrong sides together, fold both long edges of the 5 x 28-inch **COORDINATING PRINT** strips to meet in the center; press. <u>Fold in half again so the handle strips measure 1-1/4 x 28-inches; press.</u> Unfold and position a 1-1/8 x 27-inch batting strip inside of each handle strip. Fold the short ends under 1/2-inch; press. Refold the strip and edge-stitch close to the long and short folded edges.

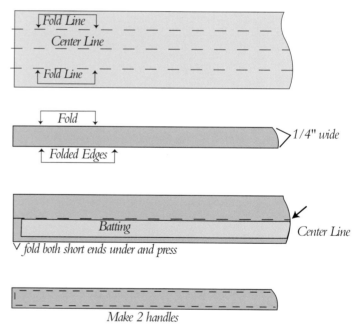

Step 7 Position the handles evenly at the top of the tote (about 3-inches from the sides), <u>inserting each end 1-inch into the tote.</u> Stitch in place.

General Instructions & Glossary

Getting Started

Yardage is based on 44-inch wide fabric. If your fabric is wider or narrower, it will affect the amount of necessary strips you need to cut in some patterns, and of course, it will affect the amount of fabric you have left over. Generally, Thimbleberries® patterns allow for a little extra fabric so you can confidently cut your pattern pieces with ease.

A rotary cutter, mat, and wide clear acrylic ruler with 1/8-inch markings are needed tools in attaining accuracy. A beginner needs good tools just as an experienced quiltmaker needs good equipment. A 24 x 36-inch cutting mat is a good size to own. It will easily accommodate the average quilt fabrics and will aid in accurate cutting. The acrylic ruler you purchase should be at least 6 x 24-inches and easy to read. Do not purchase a smaller ruler to save money. The large size will be invaluable to your quiltmaking success.

It is often recommended to prewash and press fabrics to test for colorfastness and possible shrinkage. If you choose to prewash, wash in cool water and dry in a cool to moderate dryer. Industry standards actually suggest that line drying is best. Shrinkage is generally very minimal and usually is not a concern. A good way to test your fabric for both shrinkage and colorfastness is to cut a 3-inch square of fabric. Soak the fabric in a white bowl filled with water. Squeeze the water out of the fabric and press it dry on a piece of muslin. If the fabric is going to release color, it will do so either in the water or when it is pressed dry. Remeasure the 3-inch fabric square to see if it has changed size considerably (more than 1/4-inch). If it has, wash, dry, and press the entire yardage. This little test could save you hours in prewashing and pressing.

Read instructions thoroughly before beginning a project. Each step will make more sense to you when you have a general overview of the whole process. Take one step at a time and follow the illustrations. They will often make more sense to you than the words. Take "baby steps" so you don't get overwhelmed by the entire process.

When working with flannel and other loosely woven fabrics, always prewash and dry. These fabrics almost always shrink more.

For piecing, place right sides of the fabric pieces together and use 1/4-inch seam allowances throughout the entire quilt unless otherwise specifically stated in the directions. An accurate seam allowance is the most important part of the quiltmaking process after accurately cutting. All the directions are based on accurate 1/4-inch seam allowances. It is very important to check your sewing machine to see what position your fabric should be to get accurate seams. To test, use a piece of 1/4-inch graph paper, stitch along the quarter inch line as if the paper were fabric. Make note of where the edge of the paper lines up with your presser foot or where it lines up on the throat plate of your machine. Many quilters place a piece of masking tape on the throat plate to help guide the edge of the fabric. Now test your seam allowance on fabric. Cut 2, 2-1/2-inch squares, place right sides together and stitch along one edge. Press seam allowances in one direction and measure. At this point the unit should measure 2-1/2 x 4-1/2-inches. If it does not, adjust your stitching guidelines and test again. Seam allowances are included in the cutting sizes given in this book.

Pressing is the third most important step in quiltmaking. As a general rule, you should never cross a stitched seam with another seam unless it has been pressed. Therefore, every time you stitch a seam, it needs to be pressed before adding another piece. Often, it will feel like you press as much as you sew, and often that is true. It is very important that you press and not iron the seams. Pressing is a firm, up-and-down motion that will flatten the seams but not distort the piecing. Ironing is a back-and-forth motion and will stretch and distort the small pieces. Most quilters use steam to help the pressing process. The moisture does help and will not distort the shapes as long as the pressing motion is used.

An old-fashioned rule is to press seam allowances in one direction, toward the darker fabric. Often, background fabrics are light in color and pressing toward the darker fabric prevents the seam allowances from showing through to the right side. Pressing seam allowances in one direction is thought to create a stronger seam. Also, for ease in hand quilting, the quilting lines should fall on the side of the seam which is opposite the seam allowance. As you piece quilts, you will find these "rules" to be helpful but not neccesarily always appropriate. Sometimes seams need to be pressed in the opposite direction so the seams of different units will fit together more easily, which quilters refer to as seams "nesting" together. When sewing together two units with opposing seam allowances, use the tip of your seam ripper to gently guide the units under your presser foot. Sometimes it is necessary to re-press the seams to make the units fit together nicely. Always try to achieve the least bulk in one spot and accept that no matter which way you press, it may be a little tricky and it could be a little bulky.

Pressing Direction

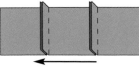

Pressing Direction

Squaring Up Blocks

To square up your blocks, first check the seam allowances. This is usually where the problem is, and it is always best to alter within the block rather than trim the outer edges. Next, make sure you have pressed accurately. Sometimes a block can become distorted by ironing instead of pressing.

To trim up block edges, use one of the many clear acrylic squares available on the market. Determine the center of the block; mark with a pin. Lay the square over the block and align as many perpendicular and horizontal lines as you can to the seams in your block. This will indicate where the block is off.

Do not trim all off on one side; this usually results in real distortion of the pieces in the block and the block design. Take a little fabric off all sides until the block is square. When assembling many blocks, it is necessary to make sure all are the same size.

Tools and Equipment

Making beautiful quilts does not require a large number of specialized tools or expensive equipment. My list of favorites is short and sweet and includes the things I use over and over again because they are always accurate and dependable.

I find a long acrylic ruler indispensable for accurate rotary cutting. The ones I like most are an Omnigrid® 6 x 24-inch grid acrylic ruler for cutting long strips and squaring up fabrics and quilt tops and a MasterPiece® 45-degree (8 x 24-inch) ruler for cutting 6- to 8-inch wide borders. I sometimes tape together two 6 x 24-inch acrylic rulers for cutting borders up to 12-inches wide.

A 15-inch Omnigrid® square acrylic ruler is great for squaring up individual blocks and corners of a quilt top, for cutting strips up to 15-inches wide or long, and for trimming side and corner triangles.

I think the markings on my 24 x 36-inch Olfa® rotary cutting mat stay visible longer than on other mats, and the lines are fine and accurate.

The largest size Olfa® rotary cutter cuts through many layers of fabric easily, and isn't cumbersome to use. The 2-1/2-inch blade slices through three layers of backing, batting, and a quilt top like butter.

An 8-inch pair of Gingher shears is great for cutting out appliqué templates and cutting fabric from a bolt or fabric scraps.

I keep a pair of 5-1/2-inch Gingher scissors by my sewing machine so it is handy for both machine work and handwork. This size is versatile and sharp enough to make large and small cuts equally well.

My Grabbit® magnetic pincushion has a surface that is large enough to hold lots of straight pins and a magnet strong enough to keep them securely in place.

Silk pins are long and thin, which means they won't leave large holes in your fabric. I like them because they increase accuracy in pinning pieces or blocks together. It is also easy to press over silk pins.

For pressing individual pieces, blocks, and quilt tops, I use an 18 x 48-inch sheet of plywood covered with several layers of cotton fiberfill and topped with a layer of muslin stapled to the back. The 48-inch length allows me to press an entire width of fabric at one time without the need to reposition it, and the square ends are better than tapered ends on an ironing board for pressing finished quilt tops.

Using Grain

The fabric you purchase still has selvage and before beginning to handle or cut your fabric, it's helpful to be able to recognize and understand its basic characteristics. Fabric is produced in the mill with identifiable grain or direction. These are: lengthwise, crosswise, and bias.

The lengthwise grain is the direction that fabric comes off the milling machine, and is parallel to the selvage. This grain of the fabric has the least stretch and the greatest strength.

The crosswise grain is the short distance that spans a bolt's 42-inch to 44-inch width. The crosswise grain, or width of grain, is between two sides called selvages. This grain of the fabric has medium stretch and medium strength.

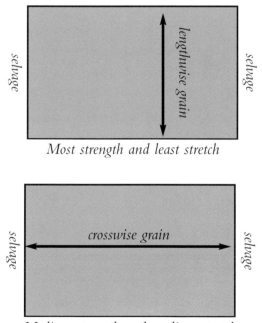

Most strength and least stretch

Medium strength and medium stretch

Avoiding Bias

The 45-degree angle on a piece of fabric is the bias and the direction with the most stretch. I suggest avoiding sewing on the bias until you're confident handling fabric. With practice and careful handling, bias edges can be sewn and are best for making curves.

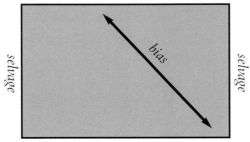

Least strength and most stretch

Rotary Cutting

SAFETY FIRST! The blades of a rotary cutter are very sharp and need to be for accurate cutting. Look at a variety of cutters to find one that feels good in your hand. All quality cutters have a safety mechanism to "close" the cutting blade when not in use. After each cut and before laying the rotary cutter down, close the blade. Soon this will become second nature to you and will prevent dangerous accidents. Always keep cutters out of the sight of children. Rotary cutters are very tempting to fiddle with when they are laying around. When your blade is dull or nicked, change it. Damaged blades do not cut accurately and require extra effort that can also result in slipping and injury. Also, always cut away from yourself for safety.

Squaring Off Fabric

Fold the fabric in half lengthwise matching the selvage edges.

Square off the ends of your fabric before measuring and cutting pieces. This means that the cut edge of the fabric must be exactly perpendicular to the folded edge which creates a 90-degree angle. Align the folded and selvage edges of the fabric with the lines on the cutting board, and place a ruled square on the fold. Place a 6 x 24-inch ruler against the side of the square to get a 90-degree angle. Hold the ruler in place, remove the square, and cut along the edge of the ruler. If you are left-handed, work from the other end of the fabric. Use the lines on your cutting board to help line up fabric, but not to measure and cut strips. Use a ruler for accurate cutting, always checking to make sure your fabric is lined up with horizontal and vertical lines on the ruler.

6 x 24" ruler

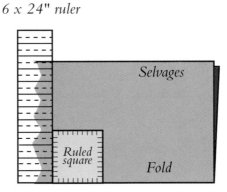

Cutting Strips

When cutting strips or rectangles, cut on the crosswise grain. Strips can then be cut into squares or smaller rectangles.

If your strips are not straight after cutting a few of them, refold the fabric, align the folded and selvage edges with the lines on the cutting board, and "square off" the edge again by trimming to straighten, and begin cutting.

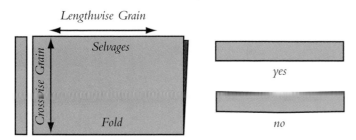

Cutting Bias Strips

When cutting bias strips, trim your yardage on the crosswise grain so the edges are straight. With right sides facing up, fold the yardage on the diagonal. Fold the selvage edge (lengthwise grain) over to meet the cut edge (crosswise grain), forming a triangle. This diagonal fold is the true bias. Position the ruler to the desired strip width from the cut edge and cut one strip. Continue moving the ruler across the fabric cutting parallel strips in the desired widths.

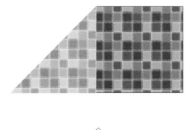

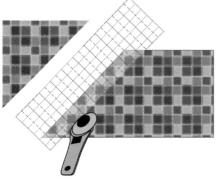

Trimming Side and Corner Triangles

In projects with side and corner triangles, the instructions have you cut side and corner triangles larger than needed. This will allow you to square up the quilt and eliminates the frustration of ending up with pre-cut side and corner triangles that don't match the size of your pieced blocks.

To cut triangles, first cut squares. The project directions will tell you what size to make the squares and whether to cut them in half to make two triangles or to cut them in quarters to make four triangles, as shown in the diagrams. This cutting method will give you side triangles that have the straight grain on the outside edges of the quilt. This is a very important part of quiltmaking that will help stabilize your quilt center.

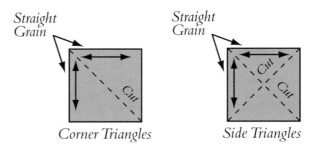

Corner Triangles   Side Triangles

Helpful Hints for Sewing with Flannel

Always prewash and machine dry flannel. This will prevent severe shrinkage after the quilt is made. Some flannels shrink more than others. For this reason, we have allowed approximately 1/4 yard extra for each fabric under the fabric requirements. Treat the more heavily napped side of solid flannels as the right side of the fabric.

Because flannel stretches more than other cotton calicos and because the nap makes them thicker, the quilt design should be simple. Let the fabric and color make the design statement.

Consider combining regular cotton calicos with flannels. The different textures complement each other nicely.

Use a 10 to 12 stitches per inch setting on your machine. A 1/4-inch seam allowance is also recommended for flannel piecing.

When sewing triangle-pieced squares together, take extra care not to stretch the diagonal seam. Trim off the points from the seam allowances to eliminate bulk.

Press gently to prevent stretching pieces out of shape.

Check block measurements as you progress. "Square up" the blocks as needed. Flannel will shift and it is easy to end up with blocks that are misshapen. If you trim and measure as you go, you are more likely to have accurate blocks. If you notice a piece of flannel is stretching more than the others, place it on the bottom when stitching on the machine. The natural action of the feed dogs will help prevent it from stretching.

Before stitching pieces, strips, or borders together, pin often to prevent fabric from stretching and moving. When stitching longer pieces together, divide the pieces into quarters and pin. Divide into even smaller sections to get more control.

Use a lightweight batting to prevent the quilt from becoming too heavy.

Cutting Triangles from Squares

Cutting accurate triangles can be intimidating for beginners, but a clear acrylic ruler, rotary cutter, and cutting mat are all that are needed to make perfect triangles. The cutting instructions often direct you to cut strips, then squares, and then triangles.

Sewing Layered Strips Together

When you are instructed to layer strips, right sides together, and sew, you need to take some precautions. Gently lay one strip on top of another, carefully lining up the raw edges. Pressing the strips together will hold them together nicely, and a few pins here and there will also help. Be careful not to stretch the strips as you sew them together.

Rod Casing or Sleeve to Hang Quilts

To hang wall quilts, attach a casing that is made of the same fabric as the quilt back. Attach this casing at the top of the quilt, just below the binding. Often, it is helpful to attach a second casing at the bottom of the quilt so you can insert a dowel into it which will help weight the quilt and make it hang free of ripples.

To make a rod casing or "sleeve," cut enough strips of fabric equal to the width of the quilt plus 2-inches for side hems. Generally, 6-inch wide strips will accommodate most rods. If you are using a rod with a larger diameter, increase the width of the strips.

Seam the strips together to get the length needed; press. Fold the strip in half lengthwise, wrong sides together. Stitch the long raw edges together with a 1/4-inch seam allowance. Center the seam on the backside of the sleeve; press. The raw edges of the seam will be concealed when the sleeve is stitched to the back of the quilt. Turn under both of the short raw edges; press and stitch to hem the ends. The final measurement should be about 1/2-inch from the quilt edges.

Pin the sleeve to the back of the quilt so the top edge of the sleeve is just below the binding. Hand stitch the top edge of the sleeve in place, then the bottom edge. Make sure to knot and secure your stitches at each end of the sleeve to make sure it will not pull away from the quilt with use. Slip the rod into the casing. If your wall quilt is not directional, making a sleeve for the bottom edge will allow you to turn your quilt end to end to relieve the stress at the top edge. You could also slip a dowel into the bottom sleeve to help anchor the lower edge of the wall quilt.

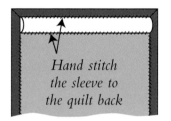

Hand stitch the sleeve to the quilt back

Hints and Helps for Pressing Strip Sets

When sewing strips of fabric together for strip sets, it is important to press the seam allowances nice and flat, usually to the darker fabric. Be careful not to stretch as you press, causing a "rainbow effect." This will affect the accuracy and shape of the pieces cut from the strip set. I like to press on the wrong side first and with the strips perpendicular to the ironing board. Then I flip the piece over and press on the right side to prevent little pleats from forming at the seams. Laying the strip set lengthwise on the ironing board seems to encourage the rainbow effect, as shown in the diagram.

Avoid this rainbow effect

Borders

NOTE: *Cut borders to the width called for. Always cut border strips a few inches longer than needed just to be safe. Diagonally piece the border strips together as needed.*

1. With pins, mark the center points along all 4 sides of the quilt. For the top and bottom borders, measure the quilt from left to right through the middle.

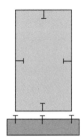

2. Measure and mark the border lengths and center points on the strips cut for the borders before sewing them on.

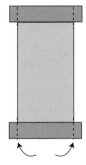

Trim away excess fabric

3. Pin the border strips to the quilt and stitch a 1/4-inch seam. Press the seam allowances toward the border. Trim off excess border lengths.

4. For the side borders, measure your quilt from top to bottom, including the borders just added, to determine the length of the side borders.

5. Measure and mark the side border lengths as you did for the top and bottom borders.

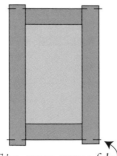

Trim away excess fabric

6. Pin and stitch the side border strips in place. Press and trim the border strips even with the borders just added.

7. If your quilt has multiple borders, measure, mark, and sew additional borders to the quilt in the same manner.

Decorative Stitches

Blanket Stitch

Outline/Stem Stitch

Straight Stitch

Choosing the Backing

The backing of any quilt is just as important to the overall design as the pieced patchwork top. Combine large-scale prints or piece coordinating fabrics together to create an interesting quilt back. Using large pieces of fabric (perhaps three different prints that are the same length as the quilt) or a large piece of fabric that is bordered by compatible prints, keeps the number of seams to a minimum, which speeds up the process. The new 108-inch wide fabric sold on the bolt eliminates the need for seaming entirely. Carefully selected fabrics for a well-constructed backing not only complement a finished quilt, but make it more useful as a reversible accent.

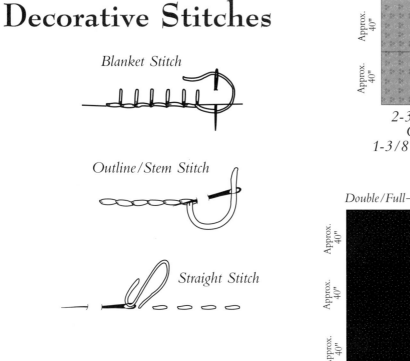

Crib— 45 x 60-inches

Approx. 40"

Approx. 40"

*2-3/4 yards
Cut 2,
1-3/8 yard lengths*

Twin—72 x 90-inches

Approx. 40"   Approx. 40"

*5-1/3 yards
Cut 2, 2-2/3 yard lengths*

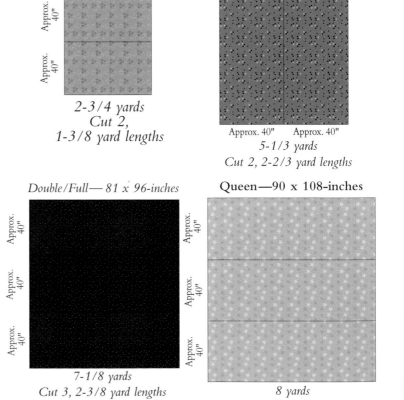

Double/Full— 81 x 96-inches

Approx. 40"

Approx. 40"

Approx. 40"

*7-1/8 yards
Cut 3, 2-3/8 yard lengths*

Queen—90 x 108-inches

Approx. 40"

Approx. 40"

Approx. 40"

*8 yards
Cut 3, 2-2/3 yard lengths*

Finishing the Quilt

1. Remove the selvages from the backing fabric. Sew the long edges together and press. Trim the backing and batting so they are 4-inches to 6-inches larger than the quilt top.

2. Mark the quilt top for quilting. Layer the backing, batting, and quilt top. Baste the 3 layers together and quilt.

3. When quilting is complete, remove basting. Hand baste all 3 layers together a scant 1/4-inch from the edge. This hand basting keeps the layers from shifting and prevents puckers from forming when adding the binding. Trim excess batting and backing fabric even with the edge of the quilt top. Add the binding as shown below.

Binding and Diagonal Piecing

1. Diagonally piece the binding strips. Fold the strip in half lengthwise, wrong sides together, and press.

Diagonal Piecing

Stitch diagonally   *Trim to 1/4-inch seam allowance*   *Press seam open*

2. Unfold and trim one end at a 45-degree angle. Turn under the edge 3/8-inch and press. Refold the strip.

Double-layer Binding

Fold line

3. With raw edges of the binding and quilt top even, stitch with a 3/8-inch seam allowance, starting 2-inches from the angled end.

4. Miter the binding at the corners. As you approach a corner of the quilt, stop sewing 3/8-inch from the corner of the quilt.

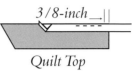

Quilt Top

5. Clip the threads and remove the quilt from under the presser foot. Flip the binding strip up and away from the quilt, then fold the binding down even with the raw edge of the quilt. Begin sewing at the upper edge. Miter all 4 corners in this manner.

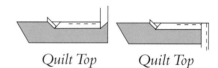

Quilt Top   *Quilt Top*

6. Trim the end of the binding so it can be tucked inside of the beginning binding about 1/2-inch. Finish stitching the seam.

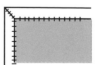

Quilt Back   *Quilt Back*

7. Turn the folded edge of the binding over the raw edges and to the back of the quilt so that the stitching line does not show. Hand sew the binding in place, folding in the mitered corners as you stitch.

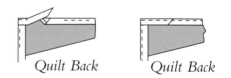

Quilt Back   *Quilt Back*   *Quilt Back*

Glossary

Appliqué The sewing technique for attaching pieces (appliqués) of fabric onto a background fabric. Appliqués may be stitched to the background by hand, using a blind stitch, or by machine, using a satin stitch or a blind hemstitch.

Backing The bottom layer of a quilt consisting of one whole piece of fabric or several fabrics joined together.

Basting The technique for joining layers of fabric or the layers of a quilt with safety pins (pin basting) or large stitches (hand basting). The pinning or stitching is temporary and is removed after permanent stitching.

Batting A layer of filler placed between two pieces of fabric to form a quilt. Its thickness and fiber content varies.

Bias The grain of woven fabric that is at a 45-degree angle to the selvages. The bias grain has more stretch and is less stable than the crosswise or lengthwise grain.

Bias strips Strips of fabric cut on the bias and joined to make one continuous strip for binding that can easily be positioned around curved edges.

Binding The strip of fabric used to cover the outside edges—top, batting and backing— of a quilt.

Block A basic unit, usually square and often repeated, of a quilt top.

Borders The framing on a quilt that serves to visually hold in the design and give the eye a stopping point.

Crosscutting Cutting fabric strips into smaller units, such as squares or rectangles.

Crosswise grain The threads running perpendicular to the selvage across the width of a woven fabric.

Cutting mat Surface used for rotary cutting that protects the tabletop and keeps the fabric from shifting while cutting. Often mats are labeled as self-healing, meaning the blade does not leave slash marks or grooves in the surface even after repeated use.

Double-fold binding Binding made from a fabric strip that is folded in half before being attached to the quilt. Also, referred to as French-fold binding.

Finished size The measurement of a completed block or quilt.

Free-motion or machine quilting A process of quilting done with the feed dogs disengaged and using a darning presser foot so the quilt can be moved freely on the machine bed in any direction.

Grain The direction of woven fabric. The crosswise grain is from selvage to selvage. The lengthwise grain runs parallel to the selvage and is stronger. The bias grain is at a 45-degree angle and has the greatest amount of stretch.

Hand quilting Series of running stitches made through all layers of a quilt with needle and thread.

Hanging sleeve Tube of fabric that is attached to the quilt back. A wooden dowel is inserted through the fabric tube to hang the quilt. It is also called a rod pocket and used with a board or rod as a support to hang a quilt on the wall.

Inner border A strip of fabric, usually more narrow than the outer border, that frames the quilt center.

Layering Placing the quilt top, batting, and quilt backing on top of each other in layers.

Lengthwise grain The threads running parallel to the selvage in a woven fabric.

Longarm quilting A quilting machine used by professional quilters in which the quilt is held taut on a frame that allows the quilter to work on a large portion of the quilt at a time. The machine head moves freely, allowing the operator to use free-motion to quilt in all directions.

Machine quilting Series of stitches made through all layers of a quilt sandwich with a sewing machine.

Marking tools A variety of pens, pencils, and chalks that can be used to mark fabric pieces or a quilt top.

Mitered seam A 45-degree angle seam.

Outer border A strip of fabric that is joined to the edges of the quilt top to finish or frame it.

Pieced border Blocks or pieced units sewn together to make a single border unit that is then sewn to the quilt center.

Piecing The process of sewing pieces of fabric together.

Pressing Using an iron with an up and down motion to set stitches and flatten a seam allowance, rather than sliding it across the fabric.

Quilt center The quilt top before borders are added.

Quilt top Top layer of a quilt usually consisting of pieced blocks.

Quilting The small running stitches made through the layers of a quilt (quilt top, batting and backing) to form decorative patterns on the surface of the quilt and hold the layers together.

Quilting stencils Quilting patterns with open areas through which a design is transferred onto a quilt top. May be purchased or made from sturdy, reusable template plastic.

Rotary cutter Tool with a sharp, round blade attached to a handle that is used to cut fabric. The blade is available in different diameters.

Rotary cutting The process of cutting fabric into strips and pieces using a revolving blade rotary cutter, a thick, clear acrylic ruler, and a special cutting mat.

Running stitches A series of in-and-out stitches used in hand quilting.

Seam allowance The 1/4-inch margin of fabric between the stitched seam and the raw edge.

Selvage The lengthwise finished edge on each side of the fabric.

Slipstitch A hand stitch used for finishing such as sewing binding to a quilt where the thread is hidden by slipping the needle between a fold of fabric and tacking down with small stitches.

Squaring up or straightening fabric The process of trimming the raw edge of the fabric so it creates a 90-degree angle with the folded edge of the fabric. Squaring up is also a term used when trimming a quilt block.

Strip sets Two or more strips of fabric, cut and sewn together along the length of the strips.

Triangle-pieced square The square unit created when two 90-degree triangles are sewn together on the diagonal.

Unfinished size The measurement of a block before the 1/4-inch seam allowance is sewn or the quilt is quilted and bound.